AVIATION LANDMARKS

They died having done something great.
How hard death must be for those who meet it having done nothing.

KOMMANDER TRYGGVE GRAN, D.F.C.

... CEVX DV "LATHAM 47"

À DIEV VAT !

AVIATION LANDMARKS

Jean Gardner

Credits

© Jean Gardner, 1990

ISBN: 0 900913 66 5

Printed in Great Britain
Designed by Gordon Ramsey
Assistant Editor, *After the Battle* magazine

PUBLISHERS
Battle of Britain Prints International Limited
Church House, Church Street
London E15 3JA
Telephone: 081-534 8833

PRINTERS
Plaistow Press Limited
Church House, Church Street
London E15 3JA

PHOTOGRAPHS
All photographs are the copyright of the author except where indicated in the author's acknowlegements.

FRONT COVER
The Royal Air Force Memorial on the Thames Embankment glows in the light of a summer dawn. Erected in 1923 to commemorate the airmen of World War I, it was re-dedicated in 1946 when Lord Trenchard unveiled an additional inscription to those of World War II. © *After the Battle*.

BACK COVER
Members of the then newly-formed Battle of Britain Fighter Association hold a Battle of Britain Day service at the Royal Air Force Memorial, led by Air Chief Marshal Lord Dowding on September 15th 1958.

FRONT ENDPAPER
The memorial to the first landing of an aeroplane on a mountain in Great Britain by Bert Hinkler and John Leeming on December 22nd, 1926 stands close to the summit of Helvellyn in the Lake District.

REAR ENDPAPER LEFT
The replacement memorial at Grafton Underwood, Northamptonshire, commemorates the 384th Bomb Group. The unveiling in October, 1985 was attended by 200 former members of the 384th, and was attended by their former Group Combat Intelligence Officer, William 'Pop' Dolan (now deceased) who unveiled the original memorial which was damaged by a heavy frost.

REAR ENDPAPER RIGHT
The four-ton granite memorial to all the Allied airmen who flew from RAF Wratting Common, Cambridgeshire, in World War II. The stone was unveiled by Air Marshal Sir Ivor Broom on May 28th, 1989.

FRONTISPIECE
One of the most dramatic of all aviation landmarks must be that to the crew of the Latham 47 which was built and launched from Cauldebec-en-Caux on the north bank of the River Seine near Rouen. The Latham 47 was lost with all crew, and the explorer Roald Amundsen, during an ill-fated search for the *Italia* airship which crashed on ice east of Spitzbergen after flying over the North Pole on a scientific expedition in 1928.

Author's Acknowledgements

I am very grateful for the help I have received from many people and organisations not acknowledged in the text. First, my thanks to my husband Cliff whose collection of aviation memorial pictures inspired me to write the book, my son Nevil whose technical advice has been invaluable, and my daughter Clare for her help with editing and research.

Friends who have been especially helpful include: Linda Hamling, Frank Ferneyhough, Gillian Thornton and Nance Darrow of Queensland who supplied details about Bert Hinkler together with the photographs.

I am indebted to Frederick Lake and his staff at the Ministry of Defence Library, and the following organisations: the Royal Air Force, the Royal Air Forces' Associations, the Air Training Corps, and the Royal Air Force Museum, Hendon.

The photographs were mainly taken by Cliff, but I would like to thank the following for their contributions: Peter Aley, Barnsley RAFA, John and Sarah Bostock, Robin Bryden, Kay Cooper, Tom Cross, George Dacam, Alan Dowsett, Arthur Evans, Gloster Saro Ltd, Peter Jervis, George Mortreuil, Ralph Mayne, RAF Northwood, Geoffrey Paine, Michael Prowse, Berry de Reus, Gordon Riley, Rolls-Royce, James Scarlett, Francis Skeat, Eric R. Smith, W. I. Taylor, Ray Warner, Alison Wightman, John Wilkie, No. 74 Squadron Roma Committee. The extract on page 34 is from *Sagittarius Rising* by Cecil Lewis, and the poem at East Kirkby on page 72 is by William Scott. Other photographs were provided from the archives of *After the Battle* magazine.

Photographs were also kindly supplied by the following: **A.E.R.E. Harwell:** 57; **Bedford County Press:** 116 left; **British Aircraft Corporation:** 108, 109; **British Airports Authority:** 37; **Central Press:** 58 top; **Daily Telegraph:** 68; **Hawker Siddeley:** 19; **HMS Daedalus:** 112; **Hull Daily Mail:** 42; **Imperial War Museum:** 34 left, 62 right; **Keystone Press Agency:** 58 bottom right; **London and Essex Guardian Newspapers:** 90 left; **Ministry of Defence:** 48, 126, 128; **Monmouth District Council Museums Service:** 18 top left; **National Air and Space Museum:** 125; **Northamptonshire Evening Telegraph:** 88; **RAE Farnborough:** 12; **RAF Museum:** 21 bottom left, 28, 31 top right, 41, 65, 71, 138 left; **Rolls-Royce:** 104; **C. F. E. Smedley/Battle of Britain Memorial Flight:** 51; **Times Newspapers:** 95.

CONTENTS

FOREWORD ———————————————————————— 6

INTRODUCTION —————————————————————— 7

1   INTO THE AIR ——————————————————— 8

2   FIRST AND FOREMOST ——————————————— 14

3   THE ARMY BEGINS TO FLY —————————————— 20

4   THE GREAT WAR ——————————————————— 28

5   THE ATLANTIC IS CONQUERED ————————————— 36

6   BY AIR TO AUSTRALIA ———————————————— 39

7   BATTLE OF BRITAIN ————————————————— 48

8   THE SECOND WORLD WAR —————————————— 54

9   COUNTING THE COST ————————————————— 58

10   LEADERS OF MEN —————————————————— 65

11   ROYAL AIR FORCE SQUADRONS ————————————— 72

12   USAAF SQUADRONS —————————————————— 84

13   THE LAST DITCH ——————————————————— 94

14   WINDOWS ON WINGS ————————————————— 102

15   ONCE AN AIRFIELD . . . ————————————————— 108

16   FURTHER AFIELD ——————————————————— 118

17   INTO THE JET AGE —————————————————— 126

18   ROUND UP ————————————————————— 130

19   THE MEN BEHIND THE MONUMENTS ———————————— 134

INDEX ——————————————————————————— 140

FOREWORD
BY AIR COMMODORE D. M. RICHARD, CBE, MRAeS

Many such as myself with a lifetime of complete immersion in aviation can perhaps be forgiven for thinking that no cloud has not been penetrated, no hangar unexplored, no aspect of aeronautics not dissected, analysed, codified or recorded.

Yet here in this delightful book, from a study of memorials, Jean Gardner has managed to encapsulate the history of aviation from the early endeavours of the pioneers, through the aerial jousting of the Great War, the trail blazing of the inter-war years, the deadly attrition of the Second World War to the more recent probing of the frontiers of Space.

Jean has succeeded in unlocking these seemingly impervious blocks of granite and letting the magnificent story of flight and human endeavour unfold. Husband Cliff was on hand to assist and one can share their enthusiasm at each new discovery. The story is told in a refreshing, innocent and disarming manner, the same qualities possessed perhaps by those young men of the skies.

In present day contemplation, it sometimes seems to me that aviation has a certain impersonal remoteness about it, being kept aloft by such things as integrated systems, in-flight procedures and cockpit resource management. This book shows the other side: of adventure, valour, sacrifice, glory and, alas, tragedy. It leaves one with a feeling of both humility and pride.

Harpenden, July 1990

INTRODUCTION

This book is based on my husband's collection of photographs of aviation memorials which currently numbers almost four hundred. Built up over the last sixteen years, it continues to expand thanks to our many friends who take a great interest in the project. When we went around the country photographing memorials and landmarks, I became increasingly aware that they revealed an ever widening picture of aviation and, as the background stories emerged, I felt that they should be recorded before the significance of some of them is lost.

The picture changes constantly as new memorials appear and others are moved or renovated. While checking details immediately prior to publication, I went to pin-point a map reference for Geoffrey de Havilland's memorial at Seven Barrows only to find that it was no longer where I had left it! Three days elapsed before I detected it about half a mile away where it had been relocated during road widening.

Even more surprising was when I arrived at Grafton Underwood only to discover a different stone altogether, the original one having split during a heavy frost. However, I was rewarded by finding the beautiful Flying Fortress window in Grafton Underwood Church which I had not come across before. Then a check on the Willian obelisk revealed that two days have inexplicably been added to the date which now reads 'SEP 8th 1912'.

New memorials have also come to my notice during the final stages of the preparation of this book. They include a plaque at the entrance to the old Handley Page airfield at Radlett, and the 'Japanese' window at RAF Coningsby.

I have not included every single memorial that we know about as some of them record similar facts. What I have done is to attempt to present the story of flight as we can see it reflected around us in the landmarks that others have been generous enough to erect for posterity.

JEAN GARDNER, 1990

M. LOUIS BLÉRIOT.

M. Louis Blériot.
FLIES by AEROPLANE from CALAIS to DOVER.
This shows the exact spot where he Landed.
Time 5.30 a.m. 25th July, 1909.
Copyright - Daily Mirror

1   INTO THE AIR

A granite silhouette of Louis Blériot's frail monoplane lies on a hillside in the shadow of Dover Castle. Twenty-three miles away on the other side of the Channel at Blériot Plage, two kilometres from Calais, stands another unique monument to his remarkable flight at the point where it started on July 25th, 1909.

This is only one aviation landmark which is permanently recorded. Much of the history of flight can be deduced from the numerous memorials marking events in aviation. Over the last sixteen years my husband Cliff and I have discovered an amazing variety of memorials in all shapes, sizes and materials. Some were very difficult to find as they are hidden in spots known only to the local people, but frequent contact with other aviation enthusiasts has produced a steady flow of information leading to new discoveries throughout the country. We have uncovered almost four hundred so far. Although some of them are crash sites this figure excludes the thousands of gravestones of airmen in cemeteries.

The audacious feats of the early balloonists' inspired the first memorials, which were followed by those to motorised flight. Many 'firsts' are recorded such as Blériot's cross-Channel flight and the crossing of the Atlantic by Alcock and Brown. Daily papers sponsored air races all over the world. In the lead was the *Daily Mail*, founded by Lord Northcliffe, who was fascinated by aviation. He offered large amounts of prize money for new achievements. Huge crowds mobbed pilots as each challenge was met.

Both world wars produced individual heroes remembered by tributes taking many different forms. The events of the Second World War gave rise to an enormous number of memorials. Aircraft of every size and shape are depicted on them and they incorporate two, three and four-bladed propellers. Most are of unique design with the exception of those to Royal Air Force squadrons in Lincolnshire. United States airmen were responsible for many which tend to be more flamboyant than the British ones. Quite often, the announcement that an airfield is to be closed or a squadron disbanded triggers the plans for a memorial.

Aviation pioneers are often immortalised. The types of memorial vary from pillars, plaques and propellers to stained glass and statues. One of the most unusual must surely be that to Frank Halford — designer of de Havilland engines — at Salisbury Hall, Hertfordshire. It is a mask of his face cast in metal from the engine cylinder heads of the Comet racer aeroplane which won the England to Australia race in 1934.

Another which is unique is also one of the earliest. This is a stone pillar surmounted by a triangular brass plate with a hinged cover, marking the spot where the Italian aeronaut, Vincenzo Lunardi, finished his remarkable voyage by balloon in 1784. Contemporary accounts give the full story of his flight. It was the wonder of the age when steam engines in industry were still considered revolutionary.

The memorials at Welham Green, *above* (at the junction of Parsonage Lane, Huggins Lane and Dellsome Lane) and Standon Green End, *below*, mark Vincenzo Lunardi's hydrogen balloon voyage on September 15th, 1784. He was employed by the Neapolitan ambassador in London and became the toast of society when news of his flight reached London. He made many more ascents in bigger and better balloons until one of his assistants was killed in an accident. Lunardi was ostracised and he returned to Italy where he continued to make flights until he died in 1806. (*TL 229056*), (*TL 365197*)

The mask in the Mosquito Aircraft Museum at Salisbury Hall, just off the old A6, a mile south-east of London Colney (itself two miles south-east of St Albans) depicts the features of Frank Halford, the brilliant engineer who designed engines ranging from the four-cylinder 65hp Cirrus for de Havilland's first Moth to the Goblin fitted in the de Havilland Vampire jet. His most famous engine was the Gipsy Six which powered the Comet racer on its world-beating flight to Australia.

He was accompanied on his ascent from the grounds of the Honourable Artillery Company in London by a dog, a cat and a pigeon. He rose to about three thousand feet and stayed in sight of the large crowd of onlookers for about an hour. Then the wind carried him northwards. Icicles formed on the balloon when he reached seven thousand feet over Barnet. At North Mymms, near Welham Green, he touched down briefly and disembarked the animals which were suffering from the cold. He ascended again rapidly and stayed airborne for another forty minutes before landing in a meadow at Standon Green End, near Ware, Hertfordshire.

The most difficult part of the landing was getting somebody to catch the rope he threw out. Farm labourers working in the meadow ran off in terror as the 'flying monster' approached them, and declared 'They would have nothing to do with one who came on the Devil's horse.' Luckily Elizabeth Brett, a servant girl, encouraged by the promise of five guineas seized the rope. She made the following affidavit next day. 'That upon going to the door of the house, I perceived a strange large body in the air; and on approaching it in a meadow near the house called Long Mead, I perceived a man in it: that the person in the machine, whom I knew not what to make of, but which the person in it called an Air Balloon, called to me to take hold of the rope, which I did accordingly. That John Mills and George Phillips, labourers with Mr Thomas Read, came up soon after, and being likewise requested to assist in holding the rope, both made their excuses, one of them, George Phillips, saying "he was too short," and John Mills saying "that he did not like it," that I continued to hold the rope till some other harvest men of Mr Benjamin Robinson, of High Cross, came up by whose assistance the machine was held down till the person got out of the machine.'

On the brass plate is an engraving of the balloon and an inscription which reads:

Let posterity Know
and Knowing be Astonished
that
on the 15th day of September 1784
Vincent Lunardi of Lucca in Tuscany
The first Aerial Traveller in Britain
Mounting from the Artillery Ground
in London
and
Traversing the region of the Air
for two hours and fifteen minutes
In this spot
Revisited the earth
on this rude Monument
for ages be recorded
That Wonderous enterprise
successfully achieved
by the powers of chemistry
and the fortitude of man
That improvement in science
which
The great Author of all Knowledge
Patronising in his providence
The invention of mankind
hath graciously permitted
to that benefit
and
his own eternal glory.

Another stone, placed at a road junction in Welham Green is near the spot where he touched down briefly. It is known as Balloon Corner.

The following year aviation arrived in Manchester. An advertisement in the *Manchester Mercury* in May 1785 offered tickets for half a guinea or five shillings to see a Mr Sadler ascend in a Grand Air Balloon from a place near John Howarth's house. The report of the flight said,

'Mr Sadler, from Oxford ascended from this town in a neat and elegant car, affixed to a grand superb air balloon. Everything being prepared with the utmost care and attention, the balloon filled gradually, without being impeded by any untoward accident or mistake. At about twenty minutes past one, the car being properly affixed and he himself seated in it, about half-a-dozen gentlemen held it down, and brought it forwards about two yards from between the poles on which it had been suspended; when, everything being properly adjusted, he ascended in a slow and majestic manner amid a vast concourse of spectators who saluted him with a grateful cheer, for the pleasure he afforded in so magnificent a sight, which he returned by politely waving his hat and flag.'

He landed about eight miles away and returned by post chaise to John Howarth's house on Long Millgate. Howarth's field has long been built over but a road running across it is named Balloon Street. A plaque on the wall of the corner of Corporation Street marks the event.

A plaque on an old workshop in the village of Brompton, near Scarborough states that it was here that Sir George Caley conducted many of his experiments. Another on Paradise House until recently the Graham Sea Training School, almost due west of Scarborough Castle, affirms Scarborough as his birth place.

Readers of Sir George Caley's papers *On Aerial Navigation*, published in 1810 doubted if heavier-than-air machines had any future. At a time when Napoleon was rampaging around Europe the British people were more concerned with keeping him across the water than flying through the air. But in 1909 Wilbur Wright wrote 'About a hundred years ago an Englishman, Sir George Caley, carried the science of flying to a point which it had never reached before and which it scarcely reached again during the last century.'

As aviation developed in the early years of this century Caley was acknowledged world wide as the inventor of the aeroplane, with over twenty aeronautical 'firsts' to his name. They included designing the first successful glider to fly — without a pilot — but incorporating the essential features of an aeroplane. By 1803 Trevithick's first steam carriage had been a success and Caley knew that he too needed a means of forward propulsion. If only the internal combustion engine had been invented he'd have been soaring through the air while Napoleon was still charging around on horseback.

It was not until the end of the 19th century that Percy Pilcher made his first brief controlled flight in a heavier than air machine at Stanford Park, near Rugby. He built his 'Bat' Glider in 1895. This was rapidly followed by the 'Gull' and the 'Hawk' in which he made flights of up to two hundred and fifty yards. He was fatally injured on 30th September 1899 due to a structural failure in the Hawk tail boom. A tall Ionic style pillar erected by the Aeronautical Society of Great Britain marks the spot. It is inscribed:

PERCY PILCHER
PIONEER OF
AVIATION
FELL HERE
SEPTEMBER 30th
1899

The memorial at Stanford Hall, Rugby, on the spot where Percy Pilcher crashed ending four years of experiments with gliders. His sister, Ella, who helped with their construction, stated that Percy was entirely wrapped up with the idea of flying from his earliest boyhood. Despite that, he spent several years at sea before devoting himself to the building of gliders. His first attempt — the Bat — made several short hops but it was not fully controllable. As he gained experience, he went on to build the Gull and Hawk, continually modifying his craft. His last flight was the final one planned at Stanford Hall as he was intending to fit an engine into a glider and attempt powered flight.

and on the back ICARO ALTERI — another Icarus. A replica of his Hawk built by apprentices from the Armstrong Whitworth Aircraft Company is on display at Stanford Hall.

At the Royal Aircraft Establishment, Farnborough, a stark leafless tree known as Cody's tree bears the following inscription at its base:

> Samuel Franklin Cody measured the thrust of his first aeroplane in 1908/9 by tying it to this tree and his flight of 1390 feet on 16th October 1908 was the first powered and sustained flight in Great Britain.

Cody was an American. He was not related to Buffalo Bill Cody of Wild West fame but affected his style of dress and long flowing hair under a wide-brimmed cowboy hat. He arrived in England with a theatrical show in 1896 but his great interest was the balloons and kites which he experimented with in his spare time. While Britons were celebrating Queen Victoria's Diamond Jubilee on the ground, Cody was flying high on his kites.

The Admiralty were very impressed by a demonstration at Portsmouth and recommended him to the Army. By 1904 Cody was established at the Military Balloon Factory at Farnborough, Hampshire. Not only did he teach the Royal Engineers what he knew about kites but he was able to show the cavalry a few tricks of horsemanship and shooting.

In 1903 Cody wrote in *Pearson's Magazine* 'I have invented an aerial machine, which although not perfect, has many successful attributes. I do not wish to assert that I have produced a flying machine in the full sense of the term, but I must confess that I have ambitions in that direction. I hope at no distant date to play an important part in the complete "Conquest of the Air".'

The public marvelled at the news of his flight in 1908, a time when many people had never seen a motor car. Aviation had arrived in Britain. The press went flying mad. Composer Ezra Read wrote *Aeroplane Waltzes with Cody*, to celebrate his great achievement. The pinnacle of his career came when he won the Military Trials with his biplane on Salisbury Plain in 1912. He died shortly afterwards while flying at Farnborough. In September 1964 a model of Cody's biplane was mounted on a pillar outside the officers' mess at Farnborough. The inscription on the plaque below it reads:

> The first aeroplane flight in Great Britain was made from this hillock by S. F. Cody on the morning of 16th October 1908. He took off in a westerly direction and flew for a distance of 1390 feet. This model was made in the workshops of the Royal Aircraft Establishment and presented by the Society of British Aerospace Companies to the Royal Air Force Officers Mess, Farnborough on the 6th September 1964.

The model, made of brass and showing the smallest details is now inside the officers' mess for safe keeping, but the plinth with its inscription remains in place.

The memorial at Eastchurch commemorates the home of the first true aircraft factory. The Short brothers produced six Wright flyers under contract to Orville and Wilbur Wright who came to Eastchurch in 1909. Working without drawings or plans, the Short brothers had not quite got it right and their first aeroplane was a failure. The second flew for over a mile, piloted by Moore-Brabazon in April 1909, earning him a *Daily Mail* prize of £1,000 and Pilot's Certificate No. 1.

2   FIRST AND FOREMOST

A memorial which is a gift to anyone looking for aviation history stands at Eastchurch on the Isle of Sheppey, Kent. Pictures in books usually show the massive central bust of Zeus but along the top of the wall flanking it, eighteen different designs of early aircraft are depicted weaving through the air. Each one is named except for a seaplane poised forever above a small pond. The box shaped planes were the successful ones, shown by the famous names over them. They include Sopwith, Cody, de Havilland, Bristol Aeroplane and of course Short Brothers so they were obviously working along the right lines.

Among the odder shapes is a Dunne biplane with no fuselage and an HP monoplane with a semi-circular wing. The aeroplanes are dwarfed by the figure of Zeus, the greatest of the Greek Gods and identified by the Romans as Jupiter, the God of the bright sky. Beneath his huge torso is the following:

THIS MEMORIAL COMMEMORATES THE FIRST HOME OF BRITISH AVIATION 1909. NEAR THIS SPOT AT LEYSDOWN EASTCHURCH (Mussel Manor) (Stonepits Farm) FLIGHTS AND EXPERIMENTS WERE MADE BY MEMBERS OF THE AERO CLUB (later ROYAL) OF GREAT BRITAIN. Also THE ESTABLISHMENT OF THE FIRST AIRCRAFT FACTORY IN GREAT BRITAIN BY SHORT BROTHERS 1909 And THE FORMATION OF THE FIRST ROYAL NAVAL AIR SERVICE STATION 1911.

On the left of the inscription is a list of aviators among them Moore-Brabazon, Rolls and Sopwith. On the right, entitled 'designers and constructors,' it includes the Short brothers, the craftsmen of Sheppey, the Royal Naval Air Service, four officers and twelve ratings.

Moore-Brabazon (later Lord Brabazon of Tara) made the first officially recognised aeroplane flight in England by a resident Englishman at Leysdown on the coast of Sheppey in April 1909, when he made three sustained flights in a French Voisin. Later that year he gained the £1,000 Daily Mail prize for the first Briton to cover a mile in a British aeroplane, a Short Wright biplane. Soon afterwards he took a pig up as a passenger to overthrow the old saying 'pigs might fly'. The Royal Aero Club of the United Kingdom awarded him Aviator Certificate No. 1 in recognition of his achievements. He joined the Royal Flying Corps in 1914 and helped to design the first aerial camera the following year. After the war he became a Member of Parliament with special interest in aviation. By 1942 he was Minister for Aircraft Production and created a peer. He was obsessed by flying. Admirers and strangers alike could easily identify his Lordship's private car by its unique number plate FLY 1.

The three Short brothers started as balloon makers in Battersea. After their move to Eastchurch, Horace, the eldest, invented the folding wing for naval aircraft which was to prove invaluable where space was limited on aircraft carriers, and he produced many biplanes during the First World War. Hugh, the youngest, concentrated on seaplanes and also produced the first stressed skin all metal aeroplane in 1919, while Oswald, the middle one, was quite carried away by balloons.

Because the safety of Britain's shores had always been the responsibility of the Royal Navy, the Royal Naval Air Service was formed to provide aerial defence. The first R.N.A.S. station was formed at Eastchurch in 1911. Although the airfield played an active part in both world wars it is chiefly famous for the 1909-1911 period of early flying which is shown in the carvings. The idea of a memorial was suggested in 1949. Winston Churchill, then Prime Minister endorsed an advertisement in *The Times* for funds to build it because he regarded Eastchurch as a cradle of British aviation.

Flying progressed rapidly. In 1909 at the close of the Edwardian era when railway engines were still considered the ultimate in fast transport, Louis Blériot, one of the most famous of the early aviators, made his epic flight across the English Channel. This convinced many sceptics that flight was possible. The historic flight is permanently recorded by slabs of granite cut to the shape of Blériot's flimsy craft. It is set in the green hillside where the aeroplane landed on July 25th below the lofty heights of Dover Castle. The inscription on the slab in the cockpit position is being worn away by the bottoms of children up to pensionable age who sit on it to 'fly' the plane, while a tricolour windsock flutters overhead. This

The Blériot memorial is on the exact spot where he landed at 5.15 a.m. on July 25th, 1909, having taken advantage of the still morning air for his flight (see page 8). He was a brilliant aviator and, by the time he joined Deperdussin during the First World War, he had designed over forty aircraft. The giant French Aerospatiale Company has grown from Blériot's small beginnings. The Prince and Princess of Wales visited the company in 1988 when the Prince was presented with a model of the monoplane which Blériot used for his first Channel crossing.

was one of the first memorials which we found while on a holiday and somehow our family holidays seemed to centre around them after that.

The following year found us in Calais looking for the other end of Blériot's flight. Blériot Plage, two kilometres along the coast road towards Boulogne, seemed a good place to start. In the middle of the small town, a stone obelisk stands by the side of the main road. Presented by L'Aero Club de France to mark the flight, it has an engraving of Blériot's plane on it.

A statue of Hubert Latham is set high on Mount Latham further along the Boulogne Road close to Cap Blanc Nez. The Anglo-Frenchman made the first attempt to fly an aeroplane across the English channel. He took off on July 19th, 1909 in an Antoinette six days before Blériot. After six miles his engine failed and he landed on the sea. He tried again on July 27th and was within one mile of Dover before being forced to put down on the water once more. The Antoinette is now in the Science Museum in London.

L'Aero Club de France acknowledged his brave attempts with a bronze figure of him wearing a flat cap, scarf and an ordinary jacket and trousers. Bullet holes are its most amazing feature. Latham has several in his chest and a large one which almost severs his left leg — probably from a cannon shell. The high concrete pedestal is peppered with small calibre bullet holes. He was literally in the wars.

The last time I saw the statue was on a late autumn afternoon. It stood out clearly against the sea with the white cliffs of Dover plainly visible across the Channel. The sun, low in the sky, cast shadows into the hundreds of shell holes which still scar the surrounding countryside — the result of the bombing of the cross-Channel gun emplacements which lie below the hillside. Now much of this area will be covered by spoil from the Channel tunnel which begins near here.

Hubert Latham — in bronze — looks out over the waters he twice strove to conquer in July 1909. Following Blériot's successful Channel crossing, Latham turned his mind to other things. He achieved the world altitude record of 1,486 feet and established a hundred kilometre distance speed record of one hour twenty-eight minutes. After he died in 1912 his many friends erected the memorial near Cap Blanc Nez with the assistance of L'Aero Club de France.

A few kilometres away in the old town of Boulogne, high above today's bustling fish market, is a plaque on the city wall near the police station. It records the balloon ascent on June 15th, 1785 of Pilâtre de Rosier, a contemporary of Vincenzo Lunardi and James Sadler. In November 1783 he was the first man ever to make a free flight in a hot air balloon. Originally, a condemned criminal was to be the guinea pig for the Montgolfier brothers who had planned to demonstrate their balloon before King Louis XVI and Queen Marie Antoinette. Rosier convinced the king that the honour of France was at stake and volunteered to make the attempt which was successful.

A young scientist, Pilâtre de Rosier, made the first manned flight in a tethered balloon in the presence of King Louis XVI and Queen Marie Antoinette in 1783. A condemned prisoner was to have made the ascent but Rosier took his place instead for the honour of France. Free flight soon followed and then Rosier, with his assistant Pierre Romain, attempted to cross the Channel. They took off from Boulogne in a hydrogen-filled balloon but disaster soon overtook them when it caught fire and exploded. Rescuers found Rosier dead and Romain about to expire. A third victim was Rosier's fiancée, Susan Dyer, who was so horrified at the scene that she collapsed and died of shock.

Back in Dover beneath the white cliffs, the Hon. C. S. Rolls' statue stands on the sea front near the Eastern Dock. The inscription states that he was the first man to 'cross the Channel and return in a single flight' on June 2nd, 1910. The statue was carved by Lady Scott, widow of the famous Antarctic explorer. The clothing is remarkably similar to Hubert Latham's with the addition of a pair of gaiters.

Known in aviation circles as C. S. Rolls, he was born the Honourable Charles Stewart Rolls, third son of Lord Llangathock of Hendre, near Monmouth, and he has at least three memorials. One of them stands in the centre of his home town of Monmouth, again showing him in flying clothes but this time holding a model aeroplane. It is surely the statue with the mostest. All four sides are heavily inscribed and took ages to copy down.

C. S. Rolls' third memorial is at Tuckton near Bournmouth where he was killed in 1910 while taking part in the festivities marking the centenary of Bournmouth's foundation. He was flying the French-built Wright biplane in which he had flown his double Channel crossing. A disc is set in stone near the spot where he was killed. On it a picture of his aircraft shows a solid looking wing but not much fuselage. Founder of the world famous car company with Henry Royce, the inscription includes the words 'pioneer motorist' and 'aviator', and 'the first Briton to die in powered flight'. He is also commemorated by a stained glass window at Eastchurch where he was among the pioneers.

Another first involved Geoffrey de Havilland. A mile south of Beacon Hill picnic area on the A34 from Newbury, Berkshire was a small granite slab set in concrete. It stated:

Geoffrey de Havilland assisted by Frank Hearle carried out his first flight in his home made aeroplane here at Seven Barrows on 10th September 1910.

The unveiling of the statue to C. S. Rolls in Agincourt Square in his home town of Monmouth by his father, Lord Llangathock, on October 19th, 1911 *above left*. The scene remains almost unchanged today, apart from the weathering of the statue to mark the passing years. *Below:* The death of Charles Rolls is commemorated by this memorial at Tuckton, Bournemouth.

This stone commemorates the Hon. CHARLES STEWART ROLLS who was killed in a flying accident near this spot on the 12th July 1910, the first Briton to die in powered flight.

The memorial was moved before the dual carriageway was built. It is now reached from a layby beside the northbound carriageway near the power lines. It stands a few yards along the Wayfarers Path.

Geoffrey de Havilland persuaded his grandfather to help him financially to build a flying machine. With the promise of £1000, he resigned his job in the design office of the Motor Omnibus Company and set out to create his first aircraft engine. It cost him £250 to have it built. Meanwhile he and his assistant Frank Hearle worked on the airframe.

Geoffrey de Havilland searched carefully for an isolated flying ground. While visiting his parents' home at Crux Easton on the Hampshire border where his father was the vicar, he came across the ideal place. Nearby at Seven Barrows, on the estate of Lord Carnarvon who was later to make headlines when he discovered the treasures of Tutankhamen, Moore-Brabazon had put up some aircraft sheds intending to take a biplane there. He changed his mind and decided to use Eastchurch. Lord Carnarvon let Geoffrey use the ground and arranged to keep the grass mown.

In December 1909 Geoffrey de Havilland and Frank Hearle took the finished machine to Seven Barrows. Geoffrey attempted to take off downhill into a light breeze. As he became airborne there was a loud crack. The wings folded and he was left sitting amid a heap of wreckage. Undaunted, the optimistic pair had a second plane ready by the summer of 1910. On Saturday, September 10th, the rarely-heard noise of an engine filled the air as Geoffrey de Havilland successfully flew for a quarter of a mile.

His subsequent career is well known. He was knighted for his services to aviation and when he died in 1965 his ashes were scattered over Beacon Hill. Lord Porchester, grandson of Lord Carnarvon who had encouraged young Geoffrey in his experiments, unveiled the memorial stone in 1966.

Geoffrey de Havilland's skill as an aircraft designer was apparent from the early days at Seven Barrows. After a short but successful spell at the Royal Aircraft Factory at Farnborough, he founded his own company in 1920. The Comet racer and later the Comet jet airliner spring to mind when his name is mentioned, but the aviation world remembers him particularly for his long series of Moths — the most famous undoubtedly the Tiger Moth. His deep interest in natural history was reflected by the names of many of his aircraft. Geoffrey de Havilland always recognised the value of his team and gave them full credit for their loyalty. The memorial at Seven Barrows acknowledges the assistance of Frank Hearle.

3 THE ARMY BEGINS TO FLY

Aldershot, always associated with the army, has a fine aviation obelisk near the Parachute Regiment headquarters. The military authorities began to consider what use aeroplanes could be to them as soon as man began to fly. One of the first indications of their interest is revealed by the obelisk's inscription:

IN MEMORY OF LIEUT. REGINALD ARCHIBALD
CAMMELL AIR BATTALION ROYAL ENGINEERS
WHO LOST HIS LIFE WHILE FLYING AN
AEROPLANE AT HENDON ON THE 17th SEPTEMBER
1911.

THIS OBELISK WAS ERECTED BY HIS BROTHER
OFFICERS IN RECOGNITION OF HIS SERVICES TO
MILITARY AVIATION.

A slightly earlier date appears on a plaque supported by a concrete plinth at Larkhill amid the vast expanse of Salisbury Plain. It boasts three aviation 'Firsts':

ON THIS SITE THE FIRST AERODROME FOR THE
ARMY WAS FOUNDED IN 1910 BY CAPT. J. D.
FULTON RFA AND MR B. G. COCKBURN THIS
LATER BECAME 2 COY AIR BN RE
THE BRITISH AND COLONIAL AEROPLANE
COMPANY FORERUNNERS OF THE BRISTOL
AEROPLANE COMPANY ESTABLISHED THEIR
FLYING SCHOOL HERE IN 1910
THE FIRST MILITARY AIR TRIALS WERE HELD
HERE IN 1912

The last brief line barely hints at a momentous event which has passed into history. The War Office Military Aeroplane Competition was announced in 1911. In the aviation world it soon became known as the Military Trials. Private manufacturers began working hard on their entries hoping to win one of the prizes which totalled £10,000.

Lieutenant Cammell commemorated at Aldershot was one of over thirty Army officers who had learned to fly privately. Those chosen for the newly-formed Royal Flying Corps in 1912 were given £75 to reimburse them for the cost of their tuition. Then military flying training was measured in hours and single pounds; now it is gauged in years and millions of pounds.

The British and Colonial Aeroplane Company was founded at Filton, Bristol, in 1910. The first aircraft — the Boxkite — by the company's designer, Mr G. H. Challenger, flew the same year and they went on to produce the famous 'Bristol' series of aircraft. However the early pioneers at Bristol could hardly have

imagined that one day the workshops at Filton would help turn out such an advanced aircraft as Concorde. The memorial plaque with its wealth of history stands in Wood Road, Larkhill, near the site of the old British and Colonial Aeroplane Company flying school on Salisbury Plain.

Thirty-two aeroplanes were entered but not all were ready when the competition began in August 1912. No secrecy surrounded aircraft trials in those days. Everyone in the aviation industry was there to watch and the public crowded in on all sides. The pilots and mechanics were accommodated in tents which flapped in the wind as it gusted across Salisbury Plain.

The first test was speed of assembly. Cody's plane was the only one which flew in. The others arrived by road and rail and a Coventry Ordnance was towed there by traction engine. They took from fifteen minutes to two hours to put together but the time mainly depended on how many men were involved.

Cody, flying the machine with the largest engine — a 120hp Austro-Daimler — was first off in the height test. He easily achieved the required five thousand feet and three hours duration but this was quickly eclipsed by a BE2 flown by Geoffrey de Havilland, who had become chief designer at the Royal Aircraft Factory at Farnborough. He reached a height of ten thousand five hundred feet which was a British record but, as a government employee, he was not eligible for any of the prize money.

The Avro Green halfway through the transport test during the military trials. Lieutenant Parke, RN, flew this Avro and, in doing so, accidently discovered how to get out of a spin. The aircraft later broke in two when he unceremoniously collided with the ground during a landing test.

Of the two landing tests the one for distance was simple enough producing efforts varying from sixty yards — a Blériot — to a hundred and nineteen yards — a Hanriot. But the second test which produced commendable results was landing in a ploughed field. This would deter many present day flyers.

There were speed tests but nothing compared with the speed with which an Avro was taken back to the factory in

UNVEILING MEMORIAL BY GEN: SMITH-DORRIEN TO CAPT LORAINE & S.SERG. WILSON (KILLED WHILST FLYING 5/7/12)

Manchester, rebuilt and returned within eight days to continue the trials after it crashed and broke its fuselage in two during the first week. In one test it went into a spin. Normally this would have been fatal but the pilot, Lieutenant Wilfred Parke, RN, recovered control and landed without injury. It was the only British machine to complete all the tests.

Bad weather continually interrupted the trials. Cody at fifty-two years old and weighing sixteen stone was as lively as ever, and organised cricket matches between the crews during the long waits for suitable conditions. He took the first prize of £4,000 in the international class and £1,500 in the class for British subjects. Ironically his biplane was not a success and he was killed flying it a few months later.

Geoffrey de Havilland provided the answer. The Military Authorities decided that his BE2 was the best design for their purposes. The BE2c, BE2d, RE7 and RE8 all used extensively by the Royal Flying Corps during the 1914-1918 war were developed from it.

Near Shrewton, barely three miles from Larkhill, stands a Celtic cross commemorating Captain Loraine and Staff Sergeant Wilson who 'Whilst flying on duty met with an accident near this spot on July 5th 1912.' Now weathered to a soft grey, it was sparkling white when unveiled by no less a person than General Smith-Dorrien, who became Commander of the Second British Army at Ypres in WWI.

The people around Larkhill were used to seeing army manoeuvres in progress but an army of the air was still a novelty when the crash involving Captain Loraine and Staff Sergeant Wilson occurred. It attracted an enormous amount of local attention. Huge crowds joined the many high-ranking officers who attended the unveiling of the memorial to both airmen at the crossroads near Shrewton. Now the cross stands almost unnoticed as the crowds hurry past it in their haste to reach Stonehenge. (*SU 099429*)

The late Major Hewetson

At Stonehenge, making the third point of a triangle with the previous two landmarks — no, not the large stones in a circle — but a more modest monument almost overgrown at the edge of a small wood, marks another crash a year later. This time a tall Celtic cross is inscribed:

MAJOR ALEXANDER WILLIAM HEWETSON 66th BATTERY ROYAL FIELD ARTILLERY WHO WAS KILLED WHILST FLYING ON THE 17th JULY 1913 NEAR THIS SPOT.

The memorial stands in Fargo Plantation, a wood situated a quarter of a mile west of Stonehenge beside the A344.

Major Hewetson was under instruction at the British and Colonial Aeroplane Company's Flying School when he crashed *top left*. It was then known as the 'Bristol' Flying School because they mainly used their own Bristol Boxkites for training. When the slender cross in memory of Major Hewetson was unveiled, *above left*, it stood on open ground, but over the years the trees of Fargo Plantation have grown up and now almost surround it *above right*. (**SU 113427**)

The accident occurred while he was practising some figure of eight turns to enable him to qualify as a pilot. Contemporary pictures show his frail craft with its nose buried in the ground and the wings broken off.

The year 1912 is the date on the memorial which started all our research. It is away from human habitation at the side of the road between Wymondley and Willian two miles from our first home in Hertfordshire and we often wondered what it commemorated. Always well kept, with the surrounding grass neatly trimmed, it frequently had a vase of fresh flowers. One day curiosity overcame us and we stopped to read:

IN MEMORY OF CAPTAIN HAMILTON AND LIEUT.
WYNESS STUART ROYAL FLYING CORPS WHO LOST
THEIR LIVES WHILST SERVING THEIR COUNTRY AS
AVIATORS
SEP 6 1912
Erected by local subscription

This must be one of the first mentions on a memorial of the fledgling Royal Flying Corps which was only formed in May 1912. Further investigation revealed that they were flying a Deperdussin monoplane which had just won a £2,000 prize in the Military Air Trials at Larkhill. Captain Hamilton was an experienced pilot who had clocked up eight thousand miles in a similar machine. They had taken off from Wallingford, Oxfordshire, to fly to Graveley, near Willian, on reconnaissance duties connected with the army manoeuvres taking place there. They were almost there when, according to eye-witnesses cutting barley in the fields below, the plane wobbled a bit, steadied and finally exploded.

The subsequent inquiry blamed engine failure for the accident. A valve rod was thought to have come loose and damaged a strut; this allowed rigging wires to slacken off causing the wings to fold up and break off. It was the first aeroplane that most local people had seen and the accident attracted a lot of attention. The *Hertfordshire Mercury* reported:

'Rarely, if ever, has a more impressive scene been witnessed in Hitchin than that which took place on Wednesday morning when the bodies of the late Captain P. Hamilton and Lieut. A. Wyness-Stuart were removed to the Railway Station for interment. Upwards of 1,000 officers and men took part, and the route from St Saviour's Church to the Railway Station was lined by thousands of spectators. All along the route blinds were drawn and flags floated at half-mast. Since the inquest on Saturday last the coffins had remained in the mortuary chapel attached to St Saviour's Church, which was visited on Tuesday night by Mr A. J. Stuart (brother of the deceased officer) and Miss Lowe (Captain Hamilton's fiancée), who placed floral tributes on the coffins.

'Shortly after 11 o'clock on Wednesday morning three squadrons of the Hants. Dorset and Wilts. Yeomanry (who were in camp at Baldock) arrived and took up positions in Radcliffe and Walsworth Roads, while the non-commissioned officers and men of the 3rd Squadron Royal Flying Corps lined the entrance to the mortuary. Following them came a detachment of forty men of the Herts Constabulary, in charge of Supt. Reed and fifty of the 1st Hertfordshire Regiment, under the command of Lieut. Ransom. Next came the band of the Hants Carabineers, followed by a detachment of two officers and fifty unmounted men of the 1st Cavalry Brigade, one officer and six men of the Royal Engineers, two officers and fifty men of the 4th Cavalry Brigade, and an officer and two gun carriages and teams of the Royal Horse Artillery. There were also contingents from the camps at Baldock and Wymondley.'

At Willian, Hertfordshire, the army manoeuvres in 1912 were part of a large-scale exercise in eastern England involving 75,000 men. Captain Hamilton and Lieutenant Wyness Stuart were part of Blue Force which was to put up a defence against the Red Force which had invaded the East Coast. They were attempting to assess the usefulness of aircraft for reconnaissance in a battle situation. The memorial, made and erected in three weeks, was placed at the roadside about half a mile from the actual point of the Deperdussin's impact so that the numerous subscribers could more conveniently come to view it. (*TL 219297*)

Captain Hamilton and Lieutenant Wyness Stuart were the first men to be killed while flying under military orders. The accident was a major news story in the western world. The front page of the *Daily Mirror* was covered by a picture of the wreckage of the Deperdussin.

A tablet was placed in Worcester Cathedral in memory of Captain Hamilton by his brother officers of the Worcester Regiment and the Royal Flying Corps.

Only four days later another fatal crash occurred, this time to Lieutenant C. A. Bettington & Second Lieutenant E. Hotchkiss at Wolvercote, just north of Oxford, where there is a small but beautiful memorial set in the wall of a bridge. A representation of their Bristol-Coanda monoplane in black set in grey and bordered with red is all made of polished granite and shows little sign of wear.

The accident was similar to the one at Graveley. Although eyewitness accounts were contradictory, an inquiry established that a structural failure caused the rigging wires to slacken and the aeroplane to break up. 2nd Lieutenant Hotchkiss was Chief Instructor and Manager of Bristol Flying School at Brooklands, Surrey. He joined the Royal Flying Corps as a reservist and was the first one to be killed. The Bristol-Coanda had also taken a prize in the Military Air Trials at Larkhill in the section for British machines.

These two crashes in September coming so soon after that of Captain Loraine and Staff Sergeant Wilson in July caused the War office to ban pilots of the Military Wing of the Royal Flying Corps from using monoplanes, although the Royal Naval Air Service continued to use them. A Committee of Inquiry was set up to find out whether they had any inherent defects. Their report was published in February 1913 clearing monoplanes but the ban coupled with an earlier statement by Louis Blériot that monoplanes suffered excessive strain when landing discouraged their manufacture. Biplanes were favoured until stronger main-spars and a better understanding of aircraft stresses were developed.

When Major Brooke-Popham, Commanding Officer of No. 3 Squadron, Royal Flying Corps, unveiled the memorial to Lieutenants Bettington and Hotchkiss in front of a vast audience, he said that despite the crash at Willian four days earlier (when Captain Hamilton and Lieutenant Wyness Stuart had been killed), Lieutenant Bettington and Second-Lieutenant Hotchkiss had not hesitated to make a similar flight. A plaque made from a panel of their crashed Bristol-Coanda recording the event can be seen in Wolvercote Parish Church.

While the military aspect of aviation was growing rapidly, civilian pilots were still pioneering, greatly encouraged by newspaper proprietors who offered large prizes for every new achievement. Lord Northcliffe blazoned the following challenge across the *Daily Mail* on April 1st, 1913:

VAST DAILY MAIL PRIZES
The Air problem
The Waterplane, Britain's Best Weapon
£5,000 — Circuit of England and Scotland
£10,000 — Flight across Atlantic
Aeroplane? Waterplane? or Airship?

We offer £10,000 to the first person who crosses the Atlantic from any point in the United States, Canada or Newfoundland to any point in Great Britain or Ireland in 72 continuous hours. The flight may be made, of course, either way across the Atlantic. The prize is open to pilots of any nationality and machines of foreign as well as British construction. New developments are coming so thick and fast that Great Britain has not a moment to lose. We want to see less national supineness and far more energetic action in this all-important matter of air defence. That the British Government should remain inert and apathetic while other powers are busy night and day in the construction of engines of war which may be used against ourselves is not in accordance with the traditions of enterprise, determination and foresight that have made the British Empire what it is.

Gustav Hamel took up the challenge. He had flown the first British Airmail between Hendon and Windsor in 1911 to celebrate the coronation of King George V. Twenty-three-and-a-half pounds of mail was flown the twenty-one miles in twelve minutes by a Blériot monoplane. A Westland Sikorsky helicopter flew the same route in 1961 to mark the Golden Jubilee of the flight. It carried twenty-three bags of mail but was only one minute faster. As he watched the helicopter land, former telegraph boy, Harry Hessey, recalled how difficult it had been fifty years previously to persuade Mr Hamel to hand over the mail because he spoke no English.

Thousands of people watched the Jubilee flight and the British Air Mail Society held a celebration dinner. A blue and white enamelled plaque was placed in Windsor Great Park where the Blériot landed. It was re-sited in 1982 and is now against the fence next to the Long Walk Gate Lodge. Hamel commissioned an aircraft for the Atlantic crossing but unfortunately he lost his life in an air crash before the plane was completed.

In stark contrast to Hamel's flight to Windsor, few people noticed one exceptional feat. On a remote beach north of Aberdeen, a plaque mounted on local granite says:

FROM THE SANDS OF CRUDEN BAY
ON THE 30th JULY 1914 THE
NORWEGIAN AVIATOR
KOMMANDER TRYGGVE GRAN D.F.C.
MADE THE FIRST CROSSING OF THE NORTH
SEA BY AIR.

It gives little hint of the courage of the man, who had been neither a Kommander, a D.F.C., nor an experienced aviator in 1914. Son of a Bergen shipbuilder and an acclaimed skier, he had sailed the South Seas in his youth. At twenty he went to the Antarctic as chief ski adviser to Captain Scott, taking part in the ill-fated expedition to the South Pole. Indeed Tryggve Gran was among the small group who found the bodies of Captain Scott and his party and erected his own skis as a cross marking the tomb.

These words from his diary give an insight into his character: 'When I saw those three poor souls the other day, I just felt that I envied them. They died having done something great. How hard death must be for those who meet it having done nothing.'

Gustav Hamel made the short flight recorded on the plaque despite very strong winds. He decided to risk the journey in order not to disappoint the spectators. Reaching Windsor Castle, he realised the danger of attempting a landing on the tree-lined East Lawn among the waiting crowds. He therefore flew past the Round Tower and scattered a flock of sheep as he landed in a wide meadow, having flown his Blériot monoplane in the sort of conditions that most flyers would try to avoid today.

Returning to Europe, he decided to become an aviator and joined Blériot's flying school. As soon as he had gained his pilot's licence in 1914, he bought a Blériot monoplane and shipped it to Cruden Bay. He wanted to be first to fly across the North Sea. Time was vital. Hostilities were looming. The German fleet had reached threatening proportions. No civil aircraft would be allowed to leave Britain after July 30th, 1914. After an abortive attempt on the 29th, he was ready to go at one o'clock on the final day, still relatively a novice flyer. He climbed through fog and suffered from air sickness before finally breaking through to clear skies at six thousand feet. Eventually he saw mountain tops piercing the clouds and landed near Stavanger after a flight of three hundred miles.

It was the longest flight over water up to that time. He received a *Daily Mail* prize and was promptly appointed a Lieutenant in Norway's infant air force. He resigned the commission to join the British Royal Flying Corps where he earned his D.F.C. After the war his career was varied. He was the navigator for the Handley Page team who went to Newfoundland to fly across the Atlantic. They gave up their attempt after the success of Alcock and Brown. Two years later he was badly injured in a car accident. Doctors declared he would never walk again but a year later he was skiing in Spitzbergen on an expedition. In 1928 he was one of the fifteen hundred rescuers who searched for the airship Italia when it disappeared over the North Pole. He wrote several books, among them *A Hero: Captain Scott's Last Journey.*

During the Second World War, following his propensity for the newest developments, he joined the traitorous Quisling group and found himself in disgrace when peace came. In 1971 aged eighty-six, he returned to Scotland and unveiled the memorial at Cruden Bay marking his North Sea crossing. The Royal Air Force had forgiven him and provided a guard of honour.

A crowd gathered at Cruden Bay near Aberdeen on July 29th, 1914 to see Tryggve Gran take off on an attempt to cross the North Sea in his secondhand Blériot, but bad weather forced him to return a few minutes later. The following day, with just a few hours to spare before the ban on civil flying took effect, only a few people saw him take off on what was to prove a completely successful flight. During the Great War, he flew with No. 39 Home Defence Squadron at Sutton's Farm, Hornchurch, one of the units formed to deal with the growing menace of the Zeppelins, as a Lieutenant (later Captain), earning the Distinguished Flying Cross in the course of his wartime career. He was the squadron's official chronicler, writing several interesting pieces on the fight against the Zeppelins.

4   THE GREAT WAR

An Avro 504A of No. 13 Reserve Squadron about to be started up at Dover in December 1916.

The Royal Air Force was yet to be created when war was declared in August 1914. Its predecessor the Royal Flying Corps took off from the cliff top at Swingate Down near Dover to support the British Expeditionary Force in France. A plain stone column bears a plaque with the Royal Flying Corps crest under which it states:

The ROYAL FLYING CORPS contingent of the 1914
BRITISH EXPEDITIONARY FORCE consisting of
Nos. 2, 3, 4 and 5 Squadrons flew from this field to
AMIENS between 13 and 15 August 1914.

Among the pilots was Lieutenant Harvey Kelly who was the first to land in France and also the first to force down a German aircraft. The memorial stands on the remains of an old hangar base. The airfield was mainly used as a ferry point for delivering aircraft to France. The first squadrons were equipped with BE2as, Avro 504s, Blériots and Farmans and the journey time for the hundred kilometres to Amiens was approximately two hours.

In the early days aircraft were mainly used for observation. Serious aerial combat was yet to come. Pilots who had known warm-hearted international comradeship during the initial

The memorial at Swingate Down stands four hundred feet above the town of Dover. The airfield it marks was essentially a ferrying ground for aircraft going to France during the First World War. New pilots were trained there to make up the heavy losses at the front, where their life expectancy was barely three weeks. Tragically some did not even survive long enough to reach France as the proximity of the cliffs caused numerous fatal accidents during training.

days of aviation were loath to start shooting each other down, but the bombing of civilians by the dreaded German Zeppelins prompted the flyers to fight with all the power their fragile craft could muster.

Air raids were unknown in Britain until December 1914 when a German aeroplane dropped a bomb near Dover Castle, but only a month later the first airship raid took place in the Yarmouth area of Norfolk. The air raids continued through the first half of 1915 demoralising the population. The first destruction of an airship in the air revived the flagging spirits of the nation. The Warneford Memorial in Brompton Cemetery, in the heart of London records:

ERECTED BY READERS OF 'THE DAILY EXPRESS'
TO COMMEMORATE THE HEROIC EXPLOIT IN
DESTROYING A ZEPPELIN AIRSHIP NEAR GHENT
ON JUNE 7 1915.

The memorial in Brompton Cemetery to Reginald Warneford, the first naval airman to be awarded the Victoria Cross when he shot down a Zeppelin over Belgium. Apprenticed to a shipping company when he was fourteen, he later joined the Royal Naval Air Service and took only three weeks to qualify as a pilot. In May 1915, he joined No. 1 Squadron in France and brought down the German airship just a month later.

The engraving on the front panel shows clouds of smoke bursting from the doomed airship and a tiny aircraft flying above it. The pilot was Flight Sub-Lieutenant Reginald Alexander John Warneford V.C., R.N.A.S., a member of the Royal Naval Air Service.

He took off from Furnes near St Pol in Belgium about 1.00 a.m. with orders to intercept two Zeppelins in the Ghent area. He soon picked up the LZ37 north of Ostend. When he tried to get above it to drop his bombs, the airship's gunners fired at his Morane monoplane. Unhurt, he withdrew to await the airship's next move and eventually, it turned south and began to lose height for landing. Warneford climbed high above it closing the gap between them. They were over Ghent and it was starting to get light. He switched off the engine and put the plane into a steep dive. It whistled unseen through the morning mists which now enshrouded the airship. From just a hundred and fifty feet above it he dropped six bombs. The resulting explosion filled the sky with flames. The Morane spun wildly in the blast of hot air. When he regained control, Warneford realised he had no petrol. He was forced to land behind enemy lines where he discovered a broken pipe, quickly repairing it and linking it to his reserve tank. He managed to take off narrowly avoiding some German soldiers. He landed near Cap Gris Nez as his fuel ran out again. The French soldiers who found him, arrested him but after checking his story, the Morane was refuelled and he was allowed to go, arriving safely at St Pol at 10.00 a.m.

The blazing Zeppelin crashed on the Convent of St Elisabeth in Ghent, killing two nuns, a child and all but one of the German crew. Warneford was immediately awarded the Victoria Cross for his heroism. The news spread rapidly. He was sent to Paris to receive the French Légion d'Honneur and attend civic receptions to celebrate his victory. He was a hero in Britain as well as France. Pictures of him filled the newspapers and adorned the windows of recruiting offices.

Sadly, ten days later, at the height of the public's acclaim, he was killed flying a Henry Farman biplane which crashed without explanation in Paris. After the war a commemorative plaque was placed in the Convent recording Flight Sub-Lieutenant Warneford's courage. Also in St Michael's Church, Highworth, Wiltshire, where generations of Warnefords had worshipped, a memorial tablet details his brief life. In October 1987 his Victoria Cross was bought by the Fleet Air Arm Museum, Yeovilton for £55,000.

Anyone visiting Brompton Cemetery to see the Warneford Memorial should take the opportunity to read the epitaph on Percy Pilcher's grave which is also there. It reads: 'Who was killed whilst experimenting with his soaring machine at Stamford (sic) Hall, Yelvertoft, October 2nd 1899 Aged 32 years.'

We heard of a plaque commemorating an airship raid on a shop at No. 61 Farringdon Road in Central London. On a cold January day we stood across the road looking for it. To our dismay the four story terraced building was being renovated. All the paintwork around the old fashioned shop front and the sash windows above it was covered in white undercoat. Workmen were busy repairing the door and there was no sign of a plaque.

'We're just too late,' Cliff said. 'It's gone.'

Suddenly a small van which had been parked outside the shop drew away and there, down at pavement level and completely covered in fresh white paint, was a plaque cast in metal which read:

THESE PREMISES
WERE TOTALLY DESTROYED
BY A
ZEPPELIN RAID
DURING THE WORLD WAR
ON
SEPTEMBER 8th 1915
REBUILT 1917

It has now been fully restored and is there for every one to see on the front of the Jean Muir Fabric Shop.

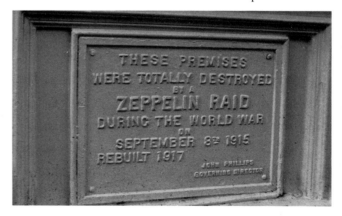

No. 61 Farringdon Road was destroyed when Zeppelins raided London, North Yorkshire and Norfolk on the night of September 8th, 1915 when a total of twenty-six people were killed and ninety-four injured.

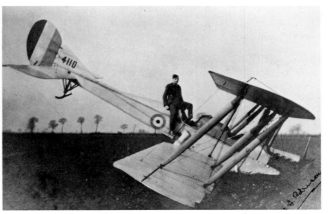

Forty people were killed and one hundred and thirty injured during a widespread Zeppelin raid in which bombs fell on Lincolnshire, Nottinghamshire, Norfolk, London and Kent on September 23rd, 1916. The villagers of Scartho, Lincolnshire, were so grateful for their good fortune in surviving unscathed that they recorded their gratitude on a memorial plaque. (*TA 265063*)

A similar plaque in stone is set in the wall of Lloyds Bank in the village of Scartho, Lincolnshire, with the following dramatic words.

A GERMAN ZEPPELIN BOMB
WAS DROPPED ON THIS SPOT
MIDNIGHT SEPT. 23RD 1916

OUR GOD MERCIFULLY PRESERVED THE INHABITANTS OF THIS VILLAGE FROM DEATH OR INJURY

OBSERVE PSALM 91

Curiosity made me read the psalm to discover that it was a discourse about the frailty and brevity of human life.

The best known airship engagement of the war was when Lieutenant William Leefe Robinson first shot one down over Britain in September 1916. It caused a sensation. Most people had believed these giant airships were impregnable with the country having been under attack by them for over a year. The idea that a flimsy biplane could destroy such a monster was almost inconceivable.

Above: **Captain Leefe Robinson sitting on a crashed BE2c of No. 39 Squadron, similar to the machine he was flying when he destroyed the Schütte-Lanz 11. His signature is just discernable in the right-hand corner. When the airship crashed at Cuffley, the nation went wild. People flocked to the spot and plundered the tangled wreckage for souvenirs. There was a brisk trade in 'pieces of the Zeppelin' and bits of twisted metal decorated many a mantelpiece. The memorial *below*, in classical style, was restored in 1986 after which it was re-dedicated during a short service of thanksgiving.**

A fleet of thirteen German airships set out to bomb London on September 2nd. Lieutenant Robinson flying a night patrol from Sutton's Farm — later Hornchurch Royal Air Force Station — in Essex, had been in the air for two hours when he saw the Schütte-Lanz 11 north-east of London. He fired two drums of ammunition along it which had no effect. Then he flew in very close and fired the whole of a third drum at one point underneath the rear. The airship burst into flames and was visible for forty miles as it fell blazing to the ground at Cuffley in Hertfordshire. The fire raged for two hours, lighting up the whole sky.

The *Daily Express* had vivid headlines the next day and their readers subscribed to a memorial at Cuffley. This was restored and re-dedicated on the 70th anniversary in September 1986. It is a tall obelisk mounted on a square plinth engraved on three sides. The front panel emblazoned by the Royal Flying Corps wings states:

ERECTED BY READERS OF 'THE DAILY EXPRESS' TO THE MEMORY OF CAPTAIN WILLIAM LEEFE ROBINSON, VC WORCS. REGT. AND RFC WHO ON SEPTEMBER 3 1916 ABOVE THIS SPOT BROUGHT DOWN SL11 THE FIRST GERMAN AIRSHIP DESTROYED ON BRITISH SOIL.

He was promoted to Captain as well as receiving the Victoria Cross for his bravery. On one side is the story of the crash and the award of the medal which King George V presented to him a few days after the event. Sadly the third side records the death of Captain Robinson at Stanmore in Middlesex on December 31st, 1918. He was fighting in France when enemy gun-fire damaged the engine of his Bristol fighter forcing him to land behind the German lines in May 1917. Despite several attempts to escape he remained a prisoner until the Armistice was signed in November 1918. When he arrived home, it was obvious to his family that he had suffered badly in captivity. He was taken ill while spending Christmas at Stanmore with his sister and died of influenza.

The crew of the SL11 were buried at Essendon two miles from Cuffley in the same churchyard as two sisters who died due to a bomb from another airship during the same raid. The airmen's bodies were later re-interred in the German War Cemetery established at Cannock, Staffordshire, in 1962.

The crews from four Zeppelins brought down in Great Britain are now buried in mass graves at Cannock: the SL11 down at Cuffley on September 3rd, 1916; the L32 at Great Burstead on September 24; the L31 at Potters Bar on October 2 and the L48 at Theberton on June 27, 1917.

There were other airship attacks after this. One is immortalised by eight stained glass windows in the parish church at Washingborough, Lincolnshire. Revenge came when a Zeppelin was shot down at Great Wigborough, Essex. A small piece of it is mounted in the arch of the church tower for all to see. Both events were in September 1916.

An even smaller memorial is on a unique wall in Postman's Park, a green oasis between the office blocks of St Martin's-le-Grand in the City of London, opposite the main Post Office. Handmade tiles each painted with the name of a brave man, woman or child cover the wall. One white with blue writing records:

ALFRED SMITH, POLICE CONSTABLE, WHO WAS
KILLED IN AN AIR RAID WHILE SAVING THE LIVES
OF WOMEN AND GIRLS JUNE 13 1917

There are no more details, but a picture of his helmet is included among the surrounding decoration.

Many stories surround Albert Ball, the first British air ace. An elaborate memorial to him stands in the castle grounds in his home town of Nottingham which is justly proud of him. His statue showing him bare headed and wearing a greatcoat rises into the trees from a classical pedestal which has these words on it:

CAPTAIN ALBERT BALL VC
7th Robin Hood Battalion Sherwood
Foresters attached Royal Flying Corps
D.S.O. two bars M.C.
Croix de Chevalier Legion d'Honneur
Order of St. George Russia
Hon. Freeman of the City of Nottingham
PER ARDUA AD ASTRA

Albert Ball was credited with forty-four aerial victories and was given 'star' treatment by the press. He crashed fatally in May 1917 but the cause remains unknown. His Victoria Cross was awarded posthumously.

The simplicity of the wording on the tile in Postman's Park conceals the horror of the daylight air raid on June 13th, 1917, which gave rise to the heaviest casualties in a single raid during the First World War. One hundred and sixty-two people were killed and four-hundred and thirty-two injured by German bombs falling on Margate in Kent, in Essex, and on London.

Cecil Lewis in *Sagittarius Rising*, his classic book about the First World War, writes of Albert Ball:

'Of the great fighting pilots his tactics were the least cunning. Absolutely fearless, the odds made no difference to him. He would always attack, single out his man, and close. On several occasions he almost rammed the enemy, and often came back with his machine shot to pieces.

'One morning, before the rest of us had gone out on patrol, we saw him coming in rather clumsily to land. He was not a stunt pilot, but flew very safely and accurately, so that, watching him, we could not understand his awkward floating landing. But when he taxied up to the sheds we saw his elevators were flapping loose — controls had been completely shot away! He had flown back from the lines and made his landing entirely by winding his adjustable tail up and down! It was incredible he had not crashed. His oil tank had been riddled, and his face and the whole nose of the machine were running with black castor oil. He was so angry at being shot up like this that he walked straight to the sheds, wiped the oil off his shoulders and face with a rag, ordered out his Nieuport, and within two hours was back with yet another Hun to his credit!

'Ball was a quiet, simple little man. His one relaxation was the violin, and his favourite after-dinner amusement was to light a red magnesium flare outside his hut and walk round it in his pyjamas, fiddling! He was meticulous in the care of his machines, guns, and in the examination of his ammunition. He never flew for amusement. The only trips he took, apart from offensive patrols, were the minimum requisite to test his engines or fire at the ground target sighting his guns. He never boasted or criticized, but his example was tremendous. . . . I believe I was the last to see him in his red-nosed SE going east at eight thousand feet. He flew straight into the white face of an enormous cloud. I followed. But when I came out on the other side, he was nowhere to be seen.'

A few days later the squadron received the news of his death. A memorial stone stands near the spot where his SE5 crashed in an isolated field which his father later bought. It is one kilometre north-east of the military cemetery near Annœullin where he was buried. A shock awaits readers of the back of the pedestal at Nottingham. Albert Ball was only twenty years old.

The solitary memorial erected by Albert Ball's father, a former Mayor of Nottingham, in the field where he crashed. As a child, Albert Ball had been keenly interested in firearms and collected pistols. He also rebuilt an old petrol engine — both occupations which no doubt helped his superb marksmanship and ability to get the best from an aero engine.

A great admirer of Albert Ball was Edward Mannock, a soldier's son. He was in the Royal Engineers but applied for a transfer to the Royal Flying Corps in 1916. With seventy-three victories to his credit he was one of the most successful British pilots of the First World War.

How he passed the army medical examination is a mystery as his left eye was virtually sightless but this did not stop him from being an excellent marksman. He arrived in France in April 1917 and had gained the Military Cross and promotion to captain by July. His tactics were superb. Contemporary accounts tell of him getting 'four kills a day'. Endlessly flying above the muddy trenches of Flanders he used to get very close to the enemy and then shoot. As one of the first Flight Commanders of No. 74 Squadron, he gave many lectures on aerial combat to the men under his command. Whereas Albert Ball was a loner, Mannock mixed constantly with his men. They were inspired by his leadership. He was a great morale booster and full of good humour.

Also in Kent, silhouetted against the sea, is a memorial which looks like a lychgate standing on the site of the old Walmer aerodrome. Beneath the small wooden roof is a board listing the names of fifteen officers of the Royal Naval Air Service who served at Walmer.

The station is chiefly remembered for its colonial connections. Walmer was needed to protect shipping in the Channel against attacks from German aircraft. Finding enough pilots was the problem. They were desperately wanted in France but a flight was essential for Walmer. The difficulty was solved by bringing back pilots who had no homes to go to when on leave for a rest at Walmer — over seventy percent of Royal Naval Air Service pilots were from overseas, mainly Canada. They enjoyed the hospitality of the local people while carrying out the patrols and having a break from front line service. At one time a lantern was lit on the anniversary of the death of each of the fifteen officers but unfortunately the custom died out.

Although he had Irish roots, he is one of over five hundred men of Canterbury whose names are inscribed on the war memorial by Christ Church gate. Inside the Cathedral, a tablet on the south wall of the nave reads:

TO THE HONOVRED MEMORY OF MAJOR EDWARD MANNOCK, VC, DSO (2 BARS), MC (1 BAR), ROYAL AIR FORCE WHO SERVED WITH EMINENT DISTINCTION IN THE GREAT WAR AND WAS KILLED JVLY 26th 1918 WHILE ENGAGED IN AERIAL COMBAT

He was awarded a posthumous Victoria Cross in 1919.

The charming and unusual memorial at Walmer commemorates officers who served on one of the earliest and smallest airfields of the First World War, now the South London Boys' Camp. A mere fifty-seven acres on Hawkshill Down, south of Walmer, it was the base for the Walmer Defence Flight whose task was to protect shipping in the Channel. The memorial was erected in 1920 by Countess Beauchamp, wife of the Lord Warden of the Cinque Ports, who lived at that time in Walmer Castle. In 1952 it was restored and moved to a more accessible location beside the Walmer to Kingsdown footpath. Lieutenant-Colonel Priestly-Bell, warden of the Boys' Camp, had the memorial restored again in 1961 and made more formal arrangements for its maintenance.

The Vickers Vimy bomber, used by Alcock and Brown in their epic crossing is preserved in the Science Museum, London.

5   THE ATLANTIC IS CONQUERED

Civil flying in Britain was permitted once more after the Air Navigation Regulations were published in April 1919. Several rival crews waited impatiently on the east coast of North America to attempt the first flight across the Atlantic Ocean. Among them were Alcock and Brown, Hawker and Grieve, Raynham and Morgan and Tryggve Gran, all well known aviators of that time. The *Daily Mail* renewed its offer of £10,000 for a successful flight. It was awarded to Alcock and Brown but none of their memorials can convey the remarkable story of their flight.

The rosy cheeked extrovert, John Alcock, known to all as Jack had been keen on flying since his school days in Manchester, when he used to make box kites and hot air balloons. He was apprenticed as a motor engineer but soon progressed to aero-engines. He became a test pilot at Brooklands, then during the First World War served in the Royal Naval Air Service at Eastchurch and in the Aegean, clocking up over four thousand flying hours by 1919.

Arthur Whitten-Brown, a slight, shy American citizen was by coincidence also brought up in Manchester. He became a British subject when war broke out in order to join the Army, but soon transferred to the Royal Flying Corps. He was shot down over France in 1915, badly injured and taken prisoner. He studied aerial navigation from books sent by the Red Cross during two years of enforced confinement. Then he was repatriated because of his wounds and went to work designing aero-engines. He met Alcock at Vickers factory at Brooklands, Surrey, soon after the Armistice. A Vickers Vimy bomber — too late for the war — was being prepared for the Atlantic crossing. Alcock was looking for a navigator and he realised immediately that he would not get a better one than Whitten-Brown.

They were soon in business. By May 1919 they were in Newfoundland with the three rival teams all determined to be first across the mighty Atlantic Ocean.

Hawker and Grieve, flying a Sopwith single engined biplane, were the first to take off on May 18th. A few hours later Raynham and Morgan followed in a Martinsyde which crashed on take-off.

The Sopwith developed engine trouble and ditched in the ocean near a Danish tramp steamer, the *Mary*. Hawker and Grieve were saved. The *Mary*, like many ships in those days, had no radio so an agonising week went by before news of their miraculous escape reached the world.

On June 14th, 1919 Alcock and Brown took off in the Vickers Vimy from Lester's Field, heading for Ireland. They endured fog, snow, ice and storms before reaching the Irish coast almost sixteen hours later. A bright green field looked a perfect landing ground but as the plane touched down they realised too late that it was a bog and the Vimy ended up on its nose.

They rescued a bag of letters containing the first Atlantic Airmail — nearly two hundred letters from St John's. Everywhere they were feted which Brown regarded as more of an ordeal than the flight. At London's Savoy Hotel, Winston Churchill presented them with the *Daily Mail* prize of £10,000 and announced that each had been awarded the O.B.E.

The bog at Clifden which they mistook for a green field is marked by a stone monument shaped like an aircraft wing and a stone cairn. They are not seen by nearly as many people as the Alcock and Brown memorials in Manchester. The people of Manchester went wild with excitement when news of the successful flight reached them. A plaque was placed in the Town Hall to commemorate the event. As Manchester's international airport has developed recently, a reminder of its early connection with flying was thought appropriate. A plaque on a plinth near the airport police station records Alcock and Brown's achievement and supports a winged figure representing flight.

The Alcock and Brown statue at Heathrow is also of recent origin but it has been moved twice since it was unveiled by Lord Brabazon in 1954. It is now at the western end of the control tower building. Both men are shown in thick sheepskin outfits, leather helmets and goggles. Arthur Brown, the shorter figure, is holding a map book.

Their Vimy was rescued from the bog but never flew again. A team from Vickers carried out repairs and presented it to the Science Museum. The small cockpit shows how cramped Alcock and Brown must have been during the flight. Their conditions compared unfavourably with the luxurious gondola attached to the R34 airship which crossed the Atlantic the following month.

On June 21st, 1979, a Royal Air Force Phantom, powered by two Rolls-Royce Spey engines, re-enacted Alcock and Brown's first transatlantic crossing. It was flown by their namesakes: Squadron Leader Tony Alcock with Flight Lieutenant W. M. Brown as navigator. The flight celebrated the 60th anniversary of the first crossing in the Rolls-Royce-powered Vickers Vimy described on the memorials at Clifden, *above right*, and Heathrow, *below right*.

The Alcock and Brown triumph eclipsed the double crossing by the R34. This great craft, nearly two hundred metres long, rose gracefully into the air on July 2nd, 1919 from its base at East Fortune on the Firth of Forth. With Major G. H. Scott of the Royal Air Force in command, it set course for the United States. Keeping very low to retain the maximum amount of hydrogen in the gas cells, it flew mainly through fog or cloud. After thirty hours a stowaway gave himself up to the captain. He was a former crew member who was left behind to save weight but his act endangered the whole voyage. When the R34 reached Mineola, New York State, after a hundred and eight hours, it had only enough fuel left for two hours flying. Favourable winds reduced the time for the return journey to Pulham in Norfolk to seventy-five hours.

This double crossing is recorded on identical plaques erected by the Air League of the British Empire. One at the entrance to East Fortune Hospital, formerly the naval air base buildings, the other at Mineola. The picture above the lettering shows the slender lines of the R34 but in no way conveys its great size. East Fortune airfield remained in service throughout the Second World War. Small civil aircraft still use the runway and there is an air museum adjacent to it.

Cardington in Bedfordshire is the best place to appreciate the size of airships. The two enormous sheds which housed the R100 and the R101 in the 1920s are an aviation landmark in their own right. They dominate the flat countryside for miles around. The crash of the R101 in 1930 was the end of airships in Britain for many years. Forty-three people perished when it crashed on a French hillside at Beauvais during a violent storm. Major G. H. Scott who had so successfully piloted the R34 across the Atlantic was among them.

An earlier disaster when the R38 broke up in the air and fell into the River Humber in 1921 had not deterred development. The forty-four people who lost their lives — thirty-two of them American — are commemorated in the Western Cemetery at Hull.

A band of airship enthusiasts still flourishes. In 1977 they erected a village sign at Pulham showing the R33 airship attached to a mooring mast. This was the craft most associated with the Airship Experimental Station at Pulham. It completed over eight hundred flying hours before being dismantled in 1928. Pulham grew up during the First World War as airships developed. They were known as Pulham Pigs because of their sausage shape. There was so much interest in them that the *Pulham Patrol*, a magazine priced 3d, was published to report their progress.

The great sheds at Cardington once housed the R100 and R101 built as part of an experimental programme to decide whether airships were practical for commercial use. The disastrous crash of the R101 settled the matter. Since the 1970s, Airship Industries have manufactured more modestly-sized dirigibles in the same sheds, their success measured by the increasing numbers seen gracefully floating over the countryside filled with sightseers. (*TL 082470*)

The Services were still building up their air strength after the First World War, experimenting with airships, seaplanes and land planes, and there was much to be discovered about navigation. In 1925 the Observer Corps was formed, little knowing what a vital part they were to play during future hostilities. Their first reporting centre was in the old post office at Cranbrook, Kent. On the building now occupying the site a memorial plaque was unveiled in 1976. The Corps badge and motto 'Forewarned is Forearmed' surmounts the following legend:

The first Royal Observer Corps Operations Room was located in this building in 1925.
THIS PLAQUE WAS ERECTED TO COMMEMORATE THE 50th ANNIVERSARY OF THE CORPS BY SERVING AND FORMER MEMBERS OF THE ROYAL OBSERVER CORPS.

It gained the 'Royal' prefix in 1941 after recognition of its sterling service during the Battle of Britain and the Blitz.

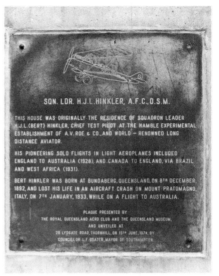

Bert Hinkler's Southampton home, *left* (and the original plaque, *right*) went to Bundaberg in 1983 by a far easier route than he took on his epic solo flight to Australia in 1928. Now the Hinkler House Museum, it displays the story of his life in Queensland as a boy, and later with No. 3 Wing of the Royal Naval Air Service, and his audacious solo flights.

6   BY AIR TO AUSTRALIA

Civilian flying was developing rapidly and in 1928 the England-Australia record was smashed by Squadron Leader H. J. L. Hinkler, otherwise Bert Hinkler. He must surely be the man with the largest variety of memorials. He was a flyer in the true tradition of pioneers.

As a boy in Queensland, Australia, he longed to fly and studied the flight of the Ibis water birds over lagoons near his home in Bundaberg. He experimented with wings strapped to his back and then built his own glider, making his first flight in it when he was nineteen. He gained practical experience of the principles and technicalities of flight while working for a flying showman, spending long hours repairing the frail craft which crashed with unfailing regularity.

He arrived in England in 1914 aged twenty-one, joining Sopwiths as a mechanic. He soon joined the Royal Naval Air Service as an Observer Gunner, gaining the Distinguished Service Medal after service in France. He received his pilot's wings in July 1918 and spent the remainder of the war with the newly-formed Royal Air Force in Italy.

Hinkler went to work for A. V. Roe in Southampton after his demobilisation and dreamed of flying to Australia. He tried and failed to do it in 1920 but did set a new long distance record in the process — nine hours for London to Turin in a light aircraft. During his years in Southampton he became chief test pilot for A. V. Roe and had a house built there which he called Mon Repos after the Queensland beach where he had tested his first homemade aeroplane. At Mon Repos he planned his flight to Australia and built an aircraft. He set many records and won several races in the twenties. One of his memorable flights is marked by a plaque beside the Wyth Path on Helvellyn in the Lake District where he made a forced landing in 1926.

His dream was fulfilled in 1928. He landed in Darwin fifteen and a half days after leaving Croydon in an Avro Avian which is now in Brisbane Museum. He almost halved the previous record of twenty-eight days held by the Australian Smith brothers. Three years later he flew from Canada to England via Brazil and West Africa establishing a South Atlantic record but finally lost his life when he crashed in Italy on his way to Australia in 1933.

A plaque was placed outside Mon Repos in Southampton on June 15th, 1974 drawing attention to Bert Hinkler's achievements but soon the house was earmarked for demolition. After a long fight to save it failed, Bundaberg Bicentennial Committee agreed at the last minute to transfer it to Bundaberg. It was dismantled brick by brick and rebuilt in the new botanic gardens on a hill overlooking Hinkler's old school, close to the lagoons where he had studied the Ibis birds as a boy. The original plaque went to Bundaberg with the house but in 1984 a new one was placed outside Hinkler Court, a block of flats which now stands on the site of Mon Repos, at Thornhill, in Southampton.

A 'Tribute to Hinkler Weekend' was held in Bundaberg as part of the Bicentennial Celebrations in June 1984. The Hinkler House Museum was opened by Sir Johannes Bjelke-Petersen, Queensland's Premier. Among the memorabilia inside is Hinkler's old *Times* Atlas which he used during his long flight and the original throttle control from the Ibis he both designed and flew. More down to earth is the kitchen sink from Mon Repos which was rescued from a council yard in Southampton. Sir Frederick Page, newly retired from British Aerospace, was responsible for the firm's gift of an Avro Avian operator's manual, one of only two known copies. He also delivered the second annual Hinkler Memorial Lecture. During the weekend's celebrations the Hinkler Commemoration Committee announced that it hoped to establish an annual aeronautical engineering bursary in memory of Bundaberg's most famous son.

More traditional memorials are a huge stone bust of Hinkler in the town showing him in flying helmet and vintage goggles, and a large black granite wall with gold lettering recording his Great Britain to Australia flight and his South Atlantic crossing. The Australia trip produced four records. The fastest time between England and Australia, the longest flight by a light aircraft, the longest solo flight and the first non-stop flight between London and Rome. He received the Air Force Cross for these achievements. Visitors flying to Bundaberg land at Hinkler Airport and are likely to dine at the Hinkler Hotel. Indeed he is the biggest thing that ever happened to Bundaberg and they are rightly proud of him.

The biggest thing to happen at Burry Port, west of Swansea in Wales, must have been the arrival of a Fokker seaplane (called 'Friendship') in the bay on June 18th, 1928. An obelisk near the old railway station records that it carried Amelia Earhart of Boston, USA, the first woman to fly across the Atlantic, with her companions Wilmur Stultz and Louis Gordon. The inscription reveals several facts. One that Amelia Earhart was an American citizen, two that the aircraft

Two other memorials to Hinkler, in his home town of Bundaberg are this stone bust, mounted on a plinth *above* and a black granite wall *below*, the reverse of which (not shown) states his principal flights as: 'First solo flight from Great Britain to Australia and first flight across South Atlantic Ocean from West to East'.

was a seaplane and three that Sir John Alcock was dead by the time of the unveiling in 1930. It conceals the fact that Amelia Earhart was only an invited passenger.

A smaller plaque under the inscription states that the monument was unveiled in August 1930 by Sir Arthur Whitten Brown, KBE, who with the late Sir John Alcock, KBE, accomplished the first aerial crossing of the Atlantic ocean on June 15th 1919.

Pilot Bill Stultz took off from Trepassey, Newfoundland, and planned to land in Ireland. After nineteen hours they were still flying in cloud and getting short of fuel. Finally they saw some fishing boats and beyond them land. They put down gratefully to discover that they had missed Ireland completely and reached Burry Port. Amelia felt that as a passenger she did not deserve all the acclaim by the press. It was not until three years later when she flew herself across in a Lockheed Vega that she felt she had earned her 'wings'. That trip ended in a field of cows in Londonderry but it earned Amelia three 'firsts'. The first Transatlantic crossing by a woman pilot, the first solo crossing by a woman and the first crossing in under sixteen hours.

She went on the usual round of promotional tours these events attracted and received the first National Geographical Society gold medal awarded to a woman. Amelia Earhart made many more notable flights before disappearing over the Pacific Ocean in 1937 during a round the world flight. She was only presumed dead after United States aircraft had made a systematic search of 100,000 square miles of ocean.

Many theories have been put forward as to why she vanished without trace despite this massive search. One of the most surprising was advanced by Fred Goerner in his book *The Search for Amelia Earhart*. He claims that she was on an espionage mission for the United States Government. He wrote of speaking to people who saw her on Saipan, the Japanese Military Headquarters which the Americans were not allowed to search, and they believed that she died in captivity.

Amy Johnson is better remembered in Britain than Amelia Earhart. Her solo flight to Australia in 1930 astounded the nation who were gripped by flying 'fever'. The event brightened the lives of thousands of people who were suffering from the unemployment and poverty of the thirties. She is honoured in her home town of Hull where a life-size statue showing her in a sheepskin flying suit, helmet and goggles stands at the entrance to the Prospect Shopping Centre. A plaque details her achievements. A bas-relief of her Gipsy Moth aircraft adorns the plinth. This tiny biplane with its open cockpit carried her half way around the world to Darwin in the steps or rather the flight path of Bert Hinkler.

Amy was an inexperienced pilot but fortunately a good engineer as many repairs were needed on route due to several

Amelia Earhart talks with the local people just after landing in Londonderry. She continued to make and break records in the air with the encouragement of her husband/businessman George Putnam, a former publisher who handled her publicity. She wrote two autobiographies and was a keen promoter of women's liberation.

Sheila Scott, who flew around the world in 1966, and won the Britannia Trophy in 1968, was the perfect choice to unveil the statue of Amy Johnson in her home town of Hull. Both women made headlines by their flying exploits but it was Amy who was the darling of the British public. She had learned to fly at Stag Lane, the old De Havilland airfield, and her flight to Australia in 1930 caused such a sensation that two hundred thousand people awaited her return to Croydon.

bad landings. She failed to beat Hinkler's record but received much more publicity. The *Daily Mail* awarded her £10,000 and organised a tour of forty towns.

She collected many flying records during her aviation career, including a solo flight to South Africa in a Puss Moth in 1932. And with her husband, Jim Mollison, a flight to Connecticut from Wales in a DH Dragon in 1933.

A plaque in the crypt of St Paul's Cathedral records the death of a hundred and seventy-three men and women of the Air Transport Auxiliary. Known as the ATA boys and girls, they were mainly pilots from pre-war flying clubs who, while not eligible for the Royal Air Force, were quite capable of ferrying aircraft. Their tasks expanded so much that they were later augmented by members of the Royal Air Force.

When war came Amy joined the Air Transport Auxiliary and was the first woman ATA pilot to be killed, when her aircraft crashed into the Thames Estuary in 1941. She was on a flight from Blackpool to Oxford in bad weather — many theories have been put forward but no one really knows how she came to be so far off course.

In the crypt of St Paul's Cathedral there is a Book of Remembrance containing the names of all the Air Transport Auxiliary pilots who died and Amy's name is among them. The ATA badge is also on her statue in Hull.

In spring 1987, a group of Amy's old ATA colleagues watched the unveiling of a plaque on Vernon Court, the flats near Hendon where she lived during her days at the airfield. Like Cody, Amy inspired the musical world. A popular song written about her called *Amy* was whistled by every errand boy on his deliveries and was definitely number one in the dance halls.

While pioneers like Amy Johnson and Amelia Earhart were attempting long distance flights all over the world, Captain Edward Fresson was pioneering flight of a more practical kind. As British families continued to struggle against hardship most of them still thought of flying as something for the birds, but he was working towards scheduled air services in the Highlands and Islands of Scotland.

In May 1984 a memorial was unveiled at Kirkwall Airport, Orkney commemorating the 50th anniversary of Captain Fresson's inaugural airmail service. He began Highland Airways Ltd in May 1933 flying passengers and newspapers from Inverness to Kirkwall. It took a year to convince the Post Office that an airmail service was practical. Piloting a de Havilland Dragon biplane, he flew from Inverness with mail on a trial basis. The contract was confirmed in December 1934 at the same time as Captain Fresson secured the first air ambulance contract. This saved sick patients from crossing the notorious Pentland Firth by boat which is enough to lay low even the fittest person. He kept the services flying all through the Second World War using unarmed aircraft with strict radio silence enforced.

(One other notable 'first' in Orkney was the landing of a plane on a moving ship when Squadron Commander E. H. Dunning of the Royal Naval Air Service flying a Sopwith Pup put down on HMS *Furious* in Scapa Flow on August 2nd, 1917.)

Captain Fresson's memorial at Kirkwall Airport shows a model of a de Havilland Dragon Rapide aircraft. It stands on a plinth with a profile view of Captain Fresson's face on a medallion above a summary of his flying record.

Military aircraft outnumbered civil ones at Kirkwall airfield during the war, when it was used as a satellite by Skeabrae, until No. 132 Squadron arrived with Spitfires in 1942. They were followed by No. 129 and finally No. 234. The Royal Navy took over in 1943 and Wildcats, Avengers, Fireflies and Swordfish replaced the Spitfires. Now BAe 748s and Britten-Norman Islanders are the commonest aircraft using the airfield. Outside the passenger lounge stands the memorial to Captain Fresson which was unveiled in 1976. (*HY 482078*)

A British Aerospace 748 arrived with a party for a commemorative lunch on the 50th anniversary and delivered a sack of mail to postman Kevin Kingston, a great grandson of the postman who received Captain Fresson's first bag of mail.

Captain Fresson's endeavours are also recognised at Inverness Airport where there is a painting of him receiving a Royal Mail pennant from the Director of Postal Services in Britain, General Sir Frederick Williamson, at the start of the airmail service.

1934 was also the year of the MacRobertson England-Australia Air Race, to celebrate the centenary of the State of Victoria. Geoffrey de Havilland, who from small beginnings brought his company through the precarious years of the depression by following a policy of gradual development, realised that the Americans would win unless he produced something revolutionary. The Comet racer was conceived. It was a low wing monoplane with two of de Havilland's latest Gipsy Six engines, designed by Frank Halford. With a range of over two thousand miles, it had the first retractable undercarriage and variable pitch propeller that the company had used.

The Comet was advertised in *Flight* and *The Aeroplane* in January 1934 as 'The de Havilland Comet, now being designed for the MacRobertson England to Australia international air race. Orders are invited for a limited number of this long distance type of racing aircraft.' It was offered at £5,000 — well below cost — and three were ordered. One by Amy and Jim Mollison, another by Bernard Rubin a motor racing driver and the third by Mr A. Edwards, a director of the fashionable London hotel Grosvenor House, to be flown by Charles Scott and Tom Campbell-Black. It was a great gamble. The three aircraft rapidly took shape in the factory at Hatfield, Hertfordshire. Test flying was compressed into weeks instead of the usual months. The entire de Havilland team was exhausted by the time they reached Mildenhall for the start. They had a desperate struggle to get the Comet's weight down to the required figure for the beginning of the race.

A crowd of over fifty thousand had gathered around the Suffolk airfield. In the darkness, society people still in evening dress jostled farm workers as they huddled together against the cold wind. The surrounding roads were jammed with traffic. Pre-race publicity had done its work. The Mollisons were the first to take off at 6.30 a.m. The others quickly followed them into the cloudy dawn sky.

Once the aircraft had taken off, all the spectators could do was wait for news. With almost no rest, Campbell-Black and

The Comet racer which won the England–Australia air race in 1934 skims the runway at British Aerospace, Hatfield, where after restoration it flew for the first time in nearly fifty years. Now part of the Shuttleworth Collection, it is displayed regularly at summer air shows.

Scott survived a tropical storm to reach Darwin first, but a faulty engine delayed them there. Frank Halford managed to telephone them. He diagnosed the trouble and they put it right before taking off for the final leg to Melbourne and winning the £10,000 prize money. They had covered 11,300 miles to Victoria in just under seventy-one hours, a remarkable effort.

The original Comet Hotel at Hatfield stands a few yards from the old de Havilland airfield which is now used by British Aerospace. Its plan follows the shape of the Comet racer in honour of the winners but only the few visitors who arrive by air can appreciate this. A fine model of the aircraft is perched on a carved column outside the hotel. Although it is a monoplane the wings are a similar shape to the earlier DH Dragon Rapide biplane which Captain Fresson flew. The name Grosvenor House is painted on the side. The original aircraft now belongs to the Shuttleworth Trust at Old Warden, Bedfordshire. It took fourteen years to restore to flying condition and made its first flight in forty-eight years at Hatfield in June 1987.

The Comet flown by Campbell-Black and Scott won the London to Australia air race in 1934. Later, with A. E. Clouston at the controls, it broke the London to Cape Town and London to New Zealand records. The model, which has an eight feet wing span, stands on a carved totem pole in front of the Comet Hotel at Hatfield. (*TL 214084*)

De Havilland features again on a remote memorial at Cairn Darnaw in Galloway, Scotland, where a Dragonfly hired by the *Daily Express* crashed in 1937. Carrying four men who were surveying a route from Renfrew to Liverpool, it struck the hillside in bad weather killing all on board. Despite the continuing bad weather a memorial was erected only twelve days after the crash. Workmen were knee deep in snow building the cairn of boulders from the hillside. Hundreds of people climbed the 1,600-foot hill for the short service and the unveiling by Lord Galloway of the grey Creetown granite plaque reading:

IN MEMORY
HERE FELL THE DAILY EXPRESS AIRPLANE
DRAGON FLY
ON FEBRUARY 2ND 1937,
WITH THE LOSS OF FOUR BRAVE MEN
HAROLD PEMBERTON
LESLIE JACKSON
REGINALD WESLEY
ARCHIBALD PHILPOTT

A lone aircraft from the Carlisle Flying Club flew over in tribute.

The same year saw the untimely death of Spitfire designer Reginald Mitchell. He is commemorated on the site of the old Supermarine works at Southampton, now overshadowed by a road bridge. A plain stone monument bears an outline of a Spitfire wing interlocked with a tail fin. Above it three views of a Spitfire are carved on the stone. One shows the exceptionally thin wings and no undercarriage visible, another the elliptical plan view of the wings and the third the familiar tail fin. Next to them is the following inscription:

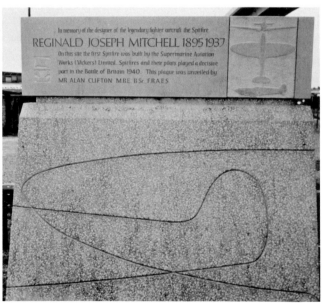

In memory of the designer of the legendary aircraft the Spitfire.
REGINALD JOSEPH MITCHELL 1895-1937
On this site the first Spitfire was built by Supermarine Aviation Works (Vickers) Ltd. Spitfires and their pilots played a decisive part in the Battle of Britain 1940.

Although he was world famous as the designer of the Spitfire, Mitchell, quiet, pipe smoking and known as a great thinker, had produced a remarkable series of seaplanes. As a young man he designed every British Schneider Trophy winner after the First World War. His Sea Lion II won the Trophy in 1922 and the Supermarine S5 won in 1927, both powered by Napier Lion engines. Mitchell turned to a new engine from Rolls-Royce to power the Supermarine S6 which

gained the 1929 race. Flight Lieutenant H. R. D. Waghorn, AFC, RAF, who piloted the winning S6 at a speed of 329 mph has his own memorial surmounted by an eagle near the Cody plinth outside the officers' mess at RAF Farnborough. He died from injuries received while testing an aircraft there in 1931. As winners for the third consecutive time, in 1931 the S6B took the Trophy outright for Great Britain.

When the Royal Air Force issued a specification for a high-speed fighter, Mitchell once again rose to the challenge. Constantly striving for perfection, he drew on all the experience gained designing seaplanes and produced the Spitfire, a single-engined monoplane. All-metal construction and stressed skin wings were among its many new features. He had been ill for several years but fortunately lived long enough to see the prototype fly successfully and be ordered by the RAF.

We cannot think of the Spitfire without the Hurricane, brainchild of Sydney Camm who began his working life as a carpenter and became one of the greatest aircraft designers. He also had the Hart, Typhoon, Tempest, Sea Fury, Hunter and Harrier to his credit. At the Royal Air Force Museum Hendon, his name is immortalised in the Sydney Camm Memorial Hall which houses several of his aircraft. He spent his early years at Martinsydes, then joined Hawkers in 1923, rising to chief designer by 1925. He modestly attributed his continued success to the skilled design team working under him. He was knighted for services to aviation in 1953 and died while still in office in 1966.

Although his design career spanned over forty years, he is best remembered for the Hurricane. It was the Royal Air Force's first monoplane fighter with retractable landing gear, fully enclosed cockpit, eight guns and a top speed of over three hundred miles an hour. It destroyed more of the enemy than any other fighter during the Battle of Britain but remains overshadowed by the more glamorous Spitfire.

A plaque fixed to the wall of the small house at No. 10 Alma Road Windsor, records the birth there of Sydney Camm in 1893. It is enhanced by a beautiful line drawing of a Hurricane. Underneath it simply says: 'Designer of the Hawker Hurricane the Battle of Britain Fighter.'

Flight Lieutenant Waghorn, who is commemorated at Farnborough, was one of those brave souls prepared to test the unknown perils of new aircraft. The Royal Aircraft Establishment ceased manufacturing aeroplanes after the First World War and it has concentrated on research work ever since. Flight Lieutenant Waghorn died from injuries received in an accident while testing new equipment on May 7th, 1931.

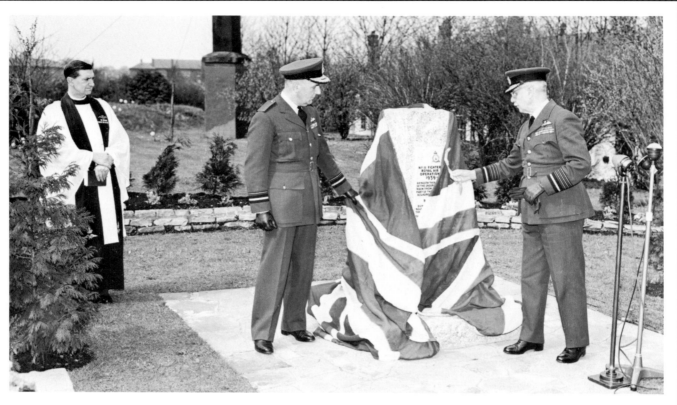

The winning strategist in one of Britain's most fateful battles, Air Chief-Marshal Lord Dowding returned to RAF Uxbridge on April 22nd, 1958 to unveil the stone marking the location of No. 11 Group's operations room.

7   BATTLE OF BRITAIN

The story of the Battle of Britain which immortalised the Spitfire and Hurricane can be deduced from innumerable landmarks, especially in south-east England. Several well publicised and 'official' memorials exist but among the lesser known is one at RAF Uxbridge revealing the enormity of the conflict. On the surface it appears to be an ordinary stone monument, however, a close inspection of the inscription discloses much more:

No. 11 FIGHTER GROUP
ROYAL AIR FORCE
OPERATIONS ROOM
1939-1946
BENEATH THIS STONE IS THE SITE OF THE
UNDERGROUND OPERATIONS ROOM FROM WHICH
THE GREATER PART OF THE HURRICANE &
SPITFIRE SQUADRONS WERE CONTROLLED
DURING THE BATTLE OF BRITAIN.
DURING THIS EPIC BATTLE THESE SQUADRONS
SHOT DOWN OVER 1,300 OF THE 1,733 ENEMY
AIRCRAFT DESTROYED.
THIS GREAT ACHIEVEMENT CONTRIBUTED
LARGELY TO OUR ULTIMATE SUCCESS AND
SURVIVAL AND INSPIRED SIR WINSTON
CHURCHILL'S NOW FAMOUS WORDS 'NEVER IN
THE FIELD OF HUMAN CONFLICT WAS SO MUCH
OWED BY SO MANY TO SO FEW.'

Since the stone was erected the operations room has been restored. It now looks exactly as it did at 11.30 a.m. on September 15th, 1940 when Winston Churchill stood in a gallery overlooking the plotting table and watched the proceedings. That day is generally accepted as the climax of the Battle of Britain. A replica of the Uxbridge Operations Room can be seen in the Royal Air Force Museum at Hendon.

The monument at Uxbridge, *above*, marks the underground headquarters of No. 11 Group which bore the brunt of the Battle of Britain. Known as 'The Hole', the Operations Room was the scene of constant activity; now it is preserved as it was at the height of the Battle (*top right*).

Sergeant Walley, formerly a fitter, qualified as a pilot and was welcomed back by his old squadron, No. 615, at Kenley in July 1940. In an air battle over Biggin Hill, the starboard wing of his Hurricane was severely damaged affecting the aircraft's controls. Sergeant Walley was seen making every possible effort to avoid built up areas before crashing on the former golf course, some twenty yards from the place where the plaque to his memory is now mounted at Merton Technical College.

The Queen's Colour Squadron, stationed at Uxbridge, mounted a guard of honour when Group Captain Leonard Cheshire unveiled a plaque commemorating a single pilot of No. 11 Fighter Group who lost his life in the Battle of Britain. Fixed to the side of Merton Technical College, South London, it is surrounded by the young people of today but honours a young man of yesterday — Sergeant Peter Walley of No. 615 Squadron who was killed when his Hurricane crashed near the spot on August 18th, 1940. His plane had been severely damaged in an air battle over Biggin Hill. The wording on the plaque tells the story: 'It is recalled with pride that knowing he was about to crash Sergeant Walley bravely managed to guide his badly damaged aircraft over nearby houses thereby safeguarding the lives of residents.'

Another unexpected place to find a memorial is at Cascades Leisure Centre, Gravesend, Kent. The Centre is built on part of the former Gravesend airfield, which opened in 1932 as a civil airport but became a satellite of Biggin Hill at the outbreak of the war. During the Battle of Britain No. 501 County of Gloucester Squadron of the Auxiliary Air Force operated from there flying Hurricanes. Early in September 1940 No. 66 Squadron moved in with their Spitfires. A plaque in the lounge area reads:

THIS SPORTS GROUND IS PART OF THE FORMER
GRAVESEND AIRPORT.
THIS PLAQUE RECORDS THE NAMES OF THOSE
MEMBERS OF THE ROYAL AIR FORCE WHO,
WHILST STATIONED HERE, GAVE THEIR LIVES
DURING THE BATTLE OF BRITAIN IN THE SUMMER
OF 1940.

Alongside are the names of fourteen men who served with the two squadrons.

Also in Kent, a solitary memorial with a chequered history has finally come to rest at Nouds Farm, near Teynham. The polished granite tribute once marked the grave of Pilot Officer Roy Marchand in Bromley Hill Cemetery. After his father's death in Switzerland, the Commonwealth War Graves Commission took over the care of the grave, erecting a standard headstone on it. Under Mr Marchand's will, the memorial was given to the London Air Museum in the 1970s but when that collection was dispersed, it was passed to the Tangmere Military Aviation Museum in Sussex.

Jim Beedle, big, round faced chairman of the museum who sadly died in April 1989, explained it to me.

'We had it on display here but it didn't seem quite the right place for it. We felt that the spot where Pilot Officer Marchand's Hurricane crashed would be more fitting. The

At one time, this impressive memorial marked the grave of Pilot Officer Roy Marchand of No. 73 Squadron. It was unveiled at the site where his Hurricane crashed, Nouds Farm, Teynham, Kent, by his daughter, Mrs Carol Ventura, on the forty-fifth anniversary of Roy's death.

local Royal Air Force Association Branch at Faversham and the owner of the farm Mr Rex Boucher were keen to have it. So it went there.'

The memorial was unveiled on September 15th, 1985, the time and date exactly forty-five years after Roy Marchand crashed at the climax of the Battle of Britain in 1940.

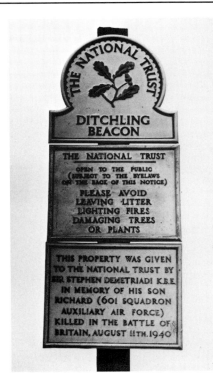

Two very different memorials connected with the Battle of Britain. *Left:* This plaque on Ditchling Beacon, Sussex, records that it was gifted to the National Trust by Sir Stephen Demetriadi in memory of his son, Richard, of No. 601 Squadron who was shot down in the sea off Portland on August 11th, 1940. His body was subsequently washed ashore in France, being buried in Cayeux-sur-Mer Communal Cemetery by the Germans. *Above:* Spitfire P7350, operated by The Battle of Britain Memorial Flight is the last flying survivor of the Battle, having served with Nos. 266 and 603 Squadrons.

While Roy Marchand's memorial marks a 'corner that is forever England,' much more than a corner of National Trust land is held in memory of Battle of Britain pilots.

One area is four acres of Ditchling Beacon, near Brighton, an ancient hill fort that must have been the scene of many earlier battles. It was left to the National Trust by industrialist Sir Stephen Demetriadi in memory of his son who was killed in the Battle of Britain. A plaque gives brief details of the bequest.

The second is recorded on a tablet of Cornish slate at Crackington Haven on the wildest part of the North Cornwall coast, where four hundred and fifty eight acres belong to the National Trust, thanks mainly to Wing Commander Parnall. He gave most of the land in memory of his brother, Flight Lieutenant Denis Parnall, and the aircrews who were killed in 1940.

The Battle of Britain Memorial Flight is widely seen each summer as it tours the airshows around the country. The Lancaster PA474 'City of Lincoln' is an impressive sight as it flies by, dwarfing the Spitfire and Hurricane which usually escort it. Three aircraft normally do the display but the Flight now has at least ten aircraft, including five Supermarine Spitfires, two Hawker Hurricanes, the Avro Lancaster, a de Havilland Chipmunk and a de Havilland Devon.

The last two are used as training aircraft. The Flight has only one pilot on its staff and otherwise relies on volunteer crews from Coningsby where it is based. The volunteer pilots need to gain experience on piston-engined tail wheel aircraft like the Chipmunk before flying the Hurricanes or Spitfires. The Flight Commander flies as captain of the Lancaster, the pride of the Flight and only airworthy example remaining in this country of over seven thousand built. It is a magnificent sight to see it fly slowly past but few of us get close enough to see the badge of the Air Gunners' Association fitted within its rear gun turret in memory of all the rear gunners who served in the Second World War.

In the Royal Air Force Chapel in Westminster Abbey, a weighty Book of Remembrance shows the vast number of men involved and at what great cost it was won. The names of both Lord Trenchard and Air Chief Marshal Dowding are engraved in the floor but it is the window glowing with vibrant colours that dominates the Chapel. The figures of four airmen in blue flying suits with yellow scarves were the first thing I noticed in the multitude of colours but gradually I realised that the rest of the window was filled with symbols from the badges of the squadrons which took part in the Battle of Britain.

Among the animal symbols, the roaring tiger of No. 74 Squadron and the elephant of No. 249 Squadron stand out while No. 66 Squadron's rattlesnake is coiled menacingly at the bottom of the window. Less noticeable are the boar's head of No. 501 Squadron and the moose head of No. 242 Squadron chosen because initially the squadron had a large number of Canadian servicemen.

Outstanding among the many winged symbols is No. 43 Squadron's cockerel. It originated before the Second World War when members of the squadron began to wear an enamelled cockerel badge used by Courage Ales as an advertising gimmick. They soon became known as 'The Fighting Cocks'. The brewery were so proud of this that many complimentary barrels of beer have been delivered to No. 43 Squadron since then.

Yorkshire and Lancashire squadrons are represented by white and red roses with No. 609 (West Riding) Squadron's white rose on crossed hunting horns the easiest to pick out. The stark white hexagon of No. 85 Squadron is conspicuous in the bottom row of glass much as it must have been to enemy planes seeing it on the side of the squadron's aircraft.

A knight's helmet and various traditional weapons and symbols bear witness of other squadrons' involvement in the conflict. Few squadron numbers are found within the designs. No. 1 Squadron's '1' is part of its badge and '303' appears in the window because the squadron was only formed in August 1940 with Polish airmen returning from Africa. They were flying Hurricanes on operations by the end of that month leaving little time for designing badges.

The vast bulk of Westminster Abbey does not diminish the tiny Royal Air Force Chapel for those who come to inspect the Roll of Honour. Here, where Lord Trenchard and Lord Dowding are buried, the glorious Battle of Britain window casts soft colours on the floor which bears their names. The chapel was dedicated on July 10th, 1947, the seventh anniversary of the 'official' beginning of the Battle, by His Majesty King George VI.

At Biggin Hill, St George's Chapel was built as a memorial to the Battle of Britain. Its plain brick lines echo the simplicity of the hut which housed the original station church. That building, dedicated as a memorial to the pilots of the Biggin Hill sector in the Battle of Britain, was unveiled by the station commander 'Sailor' Malan, who led No. 74 Squadron in the Battle and was personally credited with eighteen victories. Unfortunately it burned down in 1946.

St George's Chapel, warm and welcoming, was dedicated in 1951. Open every day it is used each Sunday for services. Visitors are encouraged to walk on the wood block floor made from propeller blades, and to examine the Book of Remembrance, the plaques and other furnishings which tell the story of the Battle of Britain.

The wooden reredos framing the altar commemorates the pilots who died during the Second World War while flying from the Biggin Hill sector. In contrast, on the altar is a mahogany lamp made by a Battle of Britain pilot who retired to Biggin Hill. The RAF station is due to close by 1992 but St George's Chapel will remain as a symbol of the part Biggin Hill played in 1940.

8 THE SECOND WORLD WAR

Another group of men who achieved hero status during the war were the Pathfinders. Brainchild of Wing Commander D. C. T. Bennett, they were formed to lead the bomber squadrons to their targets. An experienced Royal Air Force pilot, he left the service in 1935 and wrote *The Complete Air Navigator* which became the navigator's 'Bible'. When war broke out, he was flying the Atlantic route for British Overseas Airways Corporation, but was soon ferrying American aircraft across instead as his contribution to the war effort. A memorial at Gander, Newfoundland, to the Atlantic Ferry Pilots was erected when the new airport opened in 1967. A Lockheed Hudson painted in the same livery as the first one which 'Pathfinder' Bennett flew to Britain is mounted on a stone pillar with the following inscription:

ATLANTIC FERRY PILOT MEMORIAL. Air Vice Marshal D. C. T. Bennett C.B., C.B.E. and D.S.O., was the Captain of a Lockheed Hudson bomber which departed Gander 22.33 G.M.T. on the night of November 10th 1940 and landed at Aldergrove Ireland 09.45 G.M.T. the next morning. The aircraft here is identical to the one that made the flight which was the first successful Trans Atlantic crossing from Gander. It is mounted here on the site in commemoration of that event and the many thousands of men and aircraft who have followed since then — 'Better be not at all than not be noble'.

The Lockheed Hudson memorial at Gander is painted to represent T9422, the first Hudson ferried across the Atlantic to Aldergrove. This aircraft is actually BW769, an ex-45 Group, Ferry Command machine which, post war, served with Canadian Pacific Airways and Kenting Photographic Surveys.

Bennett's own memorial in Toowoomba, Queensland, where he was born, declares him to be 'an outstanding aviation pioneer, pilot, navigator, wireless operator, engineer and founder of the Pathfinder Force'. He rejoined the Royal Air Force to tackle the problem of accuracy in bombing. The Pathfinders came into being in 1942 and slowly the performance of Bomber Command improved. They are remembered in a variety of ways and places such as Pathfinder House which at first seems an odd name for District Council Offices until one realises that they were built on the site of the former headquarters of the Pathfinders in Huntingdon.

A memorial unveiled in Bexwell Parish Church in 1983 records that two men of the Pathfinders stationed at Downham Market each earned a Victoria Cross: Squadron Leader Ian Bazalgette and Flight Sergeant Arthur Aaron. During a raid on Turin, an enemy fighter attacked Flight Sergeant Aaron's Stirling bomber as it neared the target after a long flight from Britain in 1943. All the crew were either killed or wounded and the engines badly damaged in the attack. Sergeant Aaron, although mortally wounded, twice

In St Michael's Church, Coningsby, a plaque commemorates No. 83 Squadron. They played a leading role in the Pathfinder Force during the war, rapidly developing speed and accuracy in target marking. They flew from RAF Coningsby, still a front line base for the RAF. (*TF 223580*)

resumed control of the aircraft and managed to stay conscious long enough to ensure that his bomb aimer knew how to land the crippled aircraft at Bone in North Africa, despite a jammed undercarriage and a live bomb load. The surviving members of his crew owed their lives entirely to his courage.

Squadron Leader Bazalgette showed equal determination during a daylight bomber raid on a V1 rocket depot in Northern France on August 4th, 1944. The first two aircraft were badly damaged by flak. The success of the raid depended on Squadron Leader Bazalgette as he flew in to drop his markers. His Lancaster was hit several times. The starboard wing and part of the fuselage burst into flames and the bomb aimer was seriously wounded. Squadron Leader Bazalgette regained control of the plunging plane and continued his marker run, with the aircraft falling away rapidly and losing height. He maintained partial control for about thirty miles then ordered the crew to bale out. They reluctantly agreed, leaving the Squadron Leader and two wounded crewmen to attempt a landing near the village of Senantes. It was good but the plane exploded killing all three. The four who baled out were hidden by local patriots but pieced the story together after the war. Squadron Leader Bazalgette was awarded a posthumous Victoria Cross in August 1945.

No. 83 Squadron who flew as part of the Pathfinder Force from 1942 operated much of the time from Coningsby, where they were responsible for a chapel in the village church of

The unveiling of the plaque marking the site of the first VI explosion in London — on June 13th 1944 at Grove Road, Bethnal Green. It was unveiled by Lord Bottomley (on the right), from 1941-45 Deputy Regional Commissioner for South-East England, on the 41st anniversary of the event, June 13th, 1985. It was stolen almost immediately!

St. Michael. It is dedicated to all the airmen who died while flying from the station during the war. A more personal tribute is in the sergeants' mess at RAF Coningsby where a squadron badge hanging in the foyer honours members of the mess who were killed while serving with the Pathfinders of No. 83 Squadron.

In June 1988 a stained glass window in memory of all who served in the Pathfinder Force was unveiled in Guildford Cathedral. Their story is now revealed in the Royal Air Force Museum at Hendon where a permanent display of their exploits was opened in 1987 appropriately on 'Pathfinder' Bennett's birthday — September 14th.

By 1944 the Germans had developed the flying bomb and began to launch them against London. On the 41st anniversary of the first V1 attack on London, a circular blue plaque attached to the brickwork of the railway bridge in Grove Road at Bethnal Green was unveiled by Lord Bottomley stating that: 'The first flying bomb on London fell here 13th June 1944.' Unfortunately it was soon stolen but has since been replaced.

A second flying bomb incident concerned London Transport at Elmers End where a plaque on the wall of the bus garage records the names of the ten staff who were victims of one which fell there in July 1944.

Just before the first flying bomb fell at Bethnal Green, the D-Day offensive began. Harwell, now better known for its Atomic Energy Research Establishment was the scene of vital operations on June 5th, 1944. The story is summarised on a memorial pillar outside the perimeter fence of the present site. Behind it the old runway stretches into the distance. Pegasus, symbol of the Airborne Troops, is embossed above these words:

The Harwell memorial stands beside the A34, about five hundred yards from the main gate of the laboratories. Where once the aircraft mentioned in the inscription lined up, now fleets of buses stand. They bring people from a wide area to work in the huge complex of laboratories belonging to the United Kingdom Atomic Energy Research Group and the Science and Engineering Research Council.

THIS STONE MARKS THE END OF THE RUNWAY FROM WHICH AIRCRAFT OF No. 38 GROUP ROYAL AIR FORCE TOOK OFF ON THE NIGHT OF 5th JUNE 1944 WITH TROOPS OF THE 6th AIRBORNE DIVISION WHO WERE THE FIRST BRITISH SOLDIERS TO LAND IN NORMANDY IN THE MAIN ASSAULT FOR THE LIBERATION OF EUROPE.

The first to take off were six aircraft of the 22nd Independent Parachute Company who led 264 aircraft and 98 gliders of No. 38 Group. Their task was to protect the left flank of the invading Allied Armies. Sixty men in the six leading aircraft were weighed down with ammunition and equipment. They seized, marked and held landing zones for the rest of the airborne troops who were under the command of Major-General Richard Gale.

General Sir Richard Gale unveils the memorial stone to the paratroops of the 6th Airborne Division who were the first **British soldiers to land on D-Day, and the airmen of No. 38 Group, Royal Air Force, who flew them there.**

In his book *With The 6th Airborne Division In Normandy*, written when Richard Gale was a Lieutenant-General, he tells how he had the good fortune to pick a four-leafed clover while waiting for the D-Day take off. This did wonders for his morale. He admits to being superstitious because 'so much that happens baffles reason'.

In 1955 as General Sir Richard Gale he unveiled the memorial and gave it into the safe keeping of Sir John Cockcroft who promised on behalf of the Atomic Energy Research Establishment to maintain it. True to his word, it is well cared for and a Service of Remembrance is held annually.

The impressive Runnymede Memorial, unveiled by Her Majesty The Queen on October 17, 1953 (*above*).

9   COUNTING THE COST

The names of thousands of airmen and airwomen who were killed on active service are recorded on several national monuments which enlarge the picture of the importance of air power during the world wars.

At Runnymede beside the River Thames is a memorial to over twenty thousand men and women of the British and Commonwealth Air Forces who died during the Second World War and have no known graves. The six-acre site on Cooper's Hill high above the river presents a dramatic setting with views over seven counties. It seems fitting that this memorial to men and women who defended our freedom should be at the place where the Magna Carta was signed in 1215 establishing our freedom.

The white Portland stone building with green Westmorland slates on the roof is in the form of a square with a shrine opposite the triple-arched gateway and cloister linking them. Two wings curve away at the sides along the edge of the cliff. The endless panels of names in the cloisters look rather like the pages of a book with the individual alcoves forming separate chapters within it. A great feeling of spaciousness prevails and yet the alcoves of each group give a feeling of closeness. It is hard to believe that these names represent just a small percentage of those lost in the battle for air supremacy.

At Northolt, alongside the busy A40 Western Avenue, the Polish War Memorial stands appropriately at the edge of the airfield, by a pool in a paved garden. The tall white column surmounted by a bronze eagle lists Polish squadrons and battle areas, while the words

TO THE MEMORY OF FALLEN POLISH AIRMEN

are on the plinth. The surrounding curved wall has the names of over twelve thousand Polish airmen who died during flying operations from Britain. The man who was sweeping the paving the day I visited it assured me that a lot of people come to see it and spend quite a long time looking through the names and examining the inscriptions. Against the ceaseless roar of the nearby traffic, I read for the first time the words of St Paul which I shall always associate with the Polish Forces:

I HAVE FOUGHT A GOOD FIGHT,
I HAVE FINISHED MY COURSE,
I HAVE KEPT THE FAITH.

The Polish Air Force is also commemorated by a huge cross in the Polish cemetery at Newark in Nottinghamshire. This cross was erected in 1941 but later re-dedicated to include all the Polish airmen who died between 1940-1945. The cross has twelve badges of Polish squadrons on it and, like the memorial at Northolt, the words of St Paul.

After the fall of Poland in 1939, when 90 percent of their aircraft were lost with 70 percent of their aircrews, many of the survivors escaped to Britain. They provided valuable information about German tactics and reinforced the Royal Air Force when help was badly needed. They were renowned for their courage and determination to fight at any cost, as many individual memorials in this country testify.

The involvement of the men of the Fleet Air Arm in air warfare tends to be overshadowed by the Royal Navy's achievements at sea. A visit to a cold corner at Lee-on-the-Solent where a formal Portland stone memorial was erected outside the shore base of HMS *Daedelus* in 1953 gives some idea of the numbers involved. The long lists on the dark panels record the names of the men who were lost during the Second World War and have no grave but the sea.

At the beginning of the war the Fleet Air Arm was under strength and had obsolescent equipment often comprising unsuitable adaptations of land-based aircraft. This was because they had been part of the Royal Air Force who had neither sufficient resources for their own needs nor the

Northolt was the main station for the Polish airmen who had re-formed in France from those who escaped after their country was overrun in 1939. They reached these shores in time to make a vital contribution to the Battle of Britain. They were involved in the heaviest fighting and continued to serve alongside the Allied Forces throughout the war. The memorial was paid for mainly by contributions from a grateful public in recognition of the debt owed to the Polish Air Force.

experience of naval requirements. The Fleet Air Arm had a large land-based training organisation to bring the crews up to the exacting standards needed for operating from an aircraft carrier. The carrier based forces sailed with the fleets for defensive purposes and as a strike force. They also provided air support for invasions and were sometimes based ashore for operations, notably in North Africa.

The Swordfish, affectionately known as the 'Stringbag', was undoubtedly their best known plane. It was used for attacking enemy shipping, reconnaissance work, minelaying, load carrying and other duties. Lack of speed made it vulnerable but it could fly just a few feet above the sea. The pilots put this to good use as a means of defence, enticing enemy aircraft so low as they dived to attack that many of them flew straight into the water.

The Fleet Air Arm were active in the U-Boat war. Escort carriers equipped with fighters and strike aircraft sailed with the convoys cutting losses dramatically. Later in the war, they formed Strike Groups with the United States Forces using mainly American equipment in the Pacific. They operated in unfriendly seas as far apart as the South Atlantic and the Arctic Ocean; the Mediterranean and the Pacific. It is

Each year one of the most cheerful occasions at Lee-on-the-Solent is the Memorial Weekend of the Telegraphist Air Gunners Association, when veterans meet for a reunion on the Saturday evening at HMS *Daedalus*. The following day a somewhat more sombre occasion is the wreath-laying ceremony which is held at the Fleet Air Arm memorial on the seafront.

appropriate that these men who now lay forever under the sea are commemorated in Portland stone which formed under the sea millions of years ago.

East Anglia could be compared to a huge American aircraft carrier during the war because so many United States airmen were based there. The price of their sojourn is to be seen at the American Cemetery at Madingley, two miles west of Cambridge. There, the superb Memorial Chamber has an enormous map of the Atlantic and Europe illustrating the operations of US forces. It is a history lesson in itself and discloses what a tremendous rôle they undertook. The mosaic ceiling includes silhouettes of the types of American aircraft which operated from Britain. Outside, the Great Wall of the Missing bears the names of over five thousand of their servicemen with no known grave.

In December 1943 an American cemetery was activated at Cambridge to specificaly cater for the increasing number of fatalites suffered by the Eighth Air Force in carrying its air offensive to Germany. After the war it was decided to concentrate all American war dead in the United Kingdom at that location (other than those remains repatrated to the United States by the next-of-kin), and a permanent cemetary was established on 30½ acres donated by the University of Cambridge.

More American airmen are commemorated opposite the American Embassy in London's Grosvenor Square where a white obelisk was erected in 1986. The inscription reveals the identity of the 'Eagles' in the following words:

THIS MEMORIAL IS TO THE MEMORY OF THE 244 AMERICAN AND 16 BRITISH FIGHTER PILOTS AND OTHER PERSONNEL WHO SERVED IN THE THREE ROYAL AIR FORCE EAGLE SQUADRONS PRIOR TO THE PARTICIPATION OF THE UNITED STATES OF AMERICA IN THE SECOND WORLD WAR.
THEY SERVED WITH VALOUR

These were men of the calibre of Arthur Whitten-Brown who changed his nationality in order to enlist in 1914, and William Meade Lindsley Fiske III whose name is recorded on a tablet in the crypt of St Paul's Cathedral, unveiled by the then Secretary of State for Air, Sir Archibald Sinclair, on July 4th 1941 — American Independence Day. They could not wait for the United States to enter the war but volunteered their services. Just over two weeks after the outbreak of war, the first Eagle Squadron got off the ground when No. 71 Squadron was re-formed with American volunteers. Three sides of the obelisk list their names and their motto 'First from the Eyries' of which they were very proud.

The memorial to the Eagle Squadrons in Grosvenor Square is topped by a fine American bald eagle, symbol of their national pride.

The tablet in the crypt of St Paul's Cathedral recording the death of William Meade Lindsley Fiske, the first American to be killed in the Battle of Britain.

The second Eagle Squadron No. 121 came into being in May 1941 as more Americans enlisted. They have an Indian warrior's head dress on their badge and the motto 'For Liberty'. Their names are on the memorial as well as those of No. 133 Squadron which re-formed as the third Eagle Squadron as more and more Americans flocked to Britain. 'Let us to the Battle', was their motto as befits those who did not wait to be called.

These squadrons fought with the Royal Air Force, flying Hurricanes and Spitfires in sweeps over France, until September 1942 when they were transferred to become the 4th Fighter Group of the United States Army Air Force (USAAF) at Debden. This airfield in rural Essex is now an army base, but just inside the main gate a bronze plaque fixed to a granite pillar records the 4th Fighter Group's activities there. It reads:

The USAAF 4th Fighter Group recorded on the memorial at Debden built on the reputation they had gained with the Eagle Squadrons under the RAF. By the end of the war the 4th FG claimed over 1,000 enemy aircraft destroyed, but perhaps their most audacious operation occurred in March 1945 when a Mustang took off with one pilot and came back with two having landed in occupied Europe to pick up a stranded fellow pilot! (*TL 572345*)

RAF DEBDEN WAS HOME OF THE 4th FIGHTER
GROUP 8th AIR FORCE US ARMY AIR FORCE WWII
FROM SEPTEMBER 1942 TO SEPTEMBER 1945
VANGUARD YANKS OF THE 71st 121st AND 133rd RAF
EAGLE SQUADRONS AND THEIR SPITFIRES
TRADED RAF BLUES FOR US ARMY OLIVES TO
BECOME THE 4th FIGHTER GROUP.
LONG RANGING THUNDERBOLTS, LATER
MUSTANGS WERE TO HELP A DEDICATED
4th GROUP ACHIEVE THE MOST VICTORIES OVER
ENEMY AIRCRAFT IN THE ENTIRE US ARMY AIR
FORCE. 1,016 ENEMY AIRCRAFT DESTROYED.
IN REMEMBRANCE OF OUR COMRADES WHO
WERE NOT TO SEE THE WAR'S END AND OF
ANGLO-AMERICAN ENDEAVORS TO A COMMON
CAUSE, WE SURVIVORS OF THE 4th FIGHTER
GROUP, HUMBLY DEDICATE THIS MEMORIAL.

They continued as they began and were an inspiration to all the USAAF in East Anglia.

The endless lists of names on national memorials show the true cost of war. The pioneers who dreamed of flying for the masses never intended it to take this form.

In contrast, the Royal Air Force Memorial on the Thames Embankment in London has no long lists. A bronze eagle on a lofty Portland stone column is poised for flight. The site was chosen to give the impression of unfettered flight over open water. Erected in 1923 it originally commemorated the airmen of the First World War. The inscription for the Second World War casualties was added in 1946, and unveiled by Lord Trenchard.

The impressive Royal Air Force Memorial on the Thames Embankment in London seen here on a quiet Sunday morning.

Lord Trenchard (centre, with cane) inspecting the first intake at the Apprentice Training School at Halton.

10   LEADERS OF MEN

A statue of Lord Trenchard himself stands in Victoria Embankment Gardens, opposite the Royal Air Force Memorial. It shows his tall, lean figure in a greatcoat over his uniform, with a sword and a row of medals. Around the square Portland stone pedestal four metal discs are let into the base. One shows the Royal Air Force wings and the date 1918-1956, and another the badge of the Royal Scots Fusiliers where he began his service career. The third depicts palm trees and the letters WAFF 1903-1910 from his days in the West African Frontier Force, and the last one Metropolitan Police 1931-1935, a reminder of his days as Commissioner.

Although Lord Trenchard is best known in connection with the Royal Air Force, he served many years with the Royal Scots Fusiliers in India, Nigeria, South Africa and Northern Ireland. His interest in aviation awoke as he realised its potential for observing behind the enemy lines.

He was thirty-nine when he applied to join the embryo Royal Flying Corps in 1912. The War Office replied that he would have to learn to fly before he was forty. He had two weeks. A crash course in flying was called for and, with the help of the Brooklands Flying School, Trenchard accomplished the task just in time.

He was a workaholic with an unshakeable belief in flying. He was soon in charge of the Royal Flying Corps Flying

Nothing could be more appropriate than the siting of the statues of Lord Trenchard *(left)* and Lord Portal *(right)* outside the old Air Ministry building and opposite the memorial to the men of the Service they led which stands on the edge of the River Thames. Lord Trenchard inspired the pilots of the Royal Flying Corps in the First World War in France and went on to shape the Royal Air Force which Air Chief Marshal Sir Charles Portal took over in October 1940.

School at Upavon, Wiltshire, where his upright figure was often seen striding purposefully among his aircraft. His career took off rapidly. Soon after the outbreak of the First World War he was a General in charge of the Royal Flying Corps and later saw service in France. He was knighted in 1918.

Following the Armistice he became Chief of Air Staff and was promoted to Air Vice-Marshal in 1919. Air Marshal and Air Chief Marshal soon followed and he was Marshal of the Royal Air Force by 1927. During this period he created a small peacetime Air Force with little money or materials and constant opposition from the other Services. He concentrated on the standard of men selected so that he could build a high quality force which was capable of rapid expansion.

The Royal Air Force College at Cranwell for flying personnel was Lord Trenchard's idea; it opened in 1920 and he established the Apprentice Training School at Halton for technical staff. The Staff College at Andover for professional training of administrative officers soon followed.

He was deeply respected by his men despite his rather austere personality. It was his inspiring leadership which shaped the Royal Air Force that saved Britain in 1940.

Not many yards from the statue of Lord Trenchard is one of Lord Portal, the man he noticed as a future leader during their days together in the Royal Flying Corps. It is bronze and finished in a rough texture but clearly showing his decorations and sleeve rings. The head is smoothly finished and looking skywards. On the green, riven slate base, the inscription reads: 'Lord Portal of Hungerford'.

Born in 1893, Peter Portal was at Christ Church College, Oxford when the First World War broke out. He immediately rode his beloved motorcycle to the enlistment office and signed on as a despatch rider in the Royal Engineers. Eight days later he rode his machine down the platform of a London railway station and embarked for France.

He was posted to an Air Squadron (No. 3) in 1915 and became an observer. Castle Bromwich, near Birmingham, was his next stop where he learned to fly. A posting to No. 5 Squadron followed where he soon became a Flight Commander. By the end of the war he was only twenty-five years old and commanding No. 24 Wing on three stations around Grantham, Lincolnshire.

A permanent commission and training at Cranwell followed, then the new Staff College at Andover where Peter Portal was a member of the first intake. Next, a spell at the Air Ministry preceded a senior officers' course at the Royal Naval College, Greenwich, on war strategy. By 1927, and then aged thirty-nine, his work included preparing exhibitions of flying for Hendon Air Display and the Aldershot Tattoo. Then he went to Aden in 1934 as Officer Commanding British Forces before going to the Imperial Defence College as a lecturer on strategy.

By this time he had changed his name to Charles to escape the 'Peter Piper picked a peck of pickled peppers' allusion of Peter Portal. He was instrumental in the expansion of the Royal Air Force during the late thirties when the scene in Europe was darkening. Despite such a distinguished career he did not really come into the public eye until he took over as Chief of the Air Staff in 1940. He was a complete professional and bore the heavy responsibility for the Royal Air Force throughout the war. Did he sit back gracefully when he retired in 1946? No. He turned to the City of London and became a successful businessman until his death in 1971.

A third famous Royal Air Force leader was stern-faced Scotsman, Lord Dowding, who was Commander-in-Chief of Fighter Command during the Battle of Britain crisis in 1940. In the spring of 1987 the Battle of Britain Fighter Association launched a £50,000 fund-raising appeal to build a memorial to him in London. When Queen Elizabeth The Queen Mother unveiled the statue of Lord Dowding on October 30th, 1988 she recalled the days of the Battle of Britain and said how deeply appropriate it is that the memorial stands in front of St Clement Danes, the Central Church of the Royal Air Force.

Faith Winter, a Fellow of the Royal Society of British Sculptors, working on the plaster statue of Lord Dowding, *left*, used to produce the mould to cast the finished 9-foot high bronze.

Lord Dowding had been involved in flying since his days in the Royal Flying Corps during the First World War. He was a great advocate of the importance of communications and formed the Wireless Experimental Establishment at Brooklands where ground to air communications were developed. In 1930 he was attached to Supply and Development where he pressed for new aircraft for the Royal Air Force which resulted in the birth of the Spitfire and the Hurricane. As Europe moved towards war, he backed the development of radar and recommended hard runways instead of the grass strips which were customary.

From 1936 he was Commander-in-Chief of Fighter Command and devoted his time to building up the air defences which were to prove so critical in 1940. He carried the burden of Fighter Command for four years culminating in the Battle of Britain after which he was posted to the United States as an adviser on the production of military aircraft. Disputes about the rights and wrongs of his transfer will go on forever but Lord Dowding's place in history is secure as the man who successfully led his men in one of this country's most decisive battles.

He was an inspiration to the pupils of St Ninians School in Moffat which his father founded and where the young Hugh was a pupil. A tablet in the school chapel included this message: 'In prayer that the boys of his old school in their several generations might learn from his selfless service to his country'. The school closed in 1979, but the building has since been converted into sheltered housing for men and women who served in the Second World War and is known as Dowding House.

Left: **Queen Elizabeth The Queen Mother accompanied by Air Chief Marshal Sir Christopher Foxley-Norris, GCB, DSO, OBE,** in front of the newly-unveiled statue by Faith Winter. St Clement Danes is in the background.

He has long been commemorated in his home town of Moffat in Scotland, by a superb memorial which is well worth a visit during a journey north. Built from red Dumfries sandstone, it is situated in a public park. Three steps lead up to a dais, where two quadrant shaped wings enhance a central wall standing on it. Lord Dowding's portrait is in bas-relief on a bronze plaque mounted on the wall above the following words:

WITH A NATION'S GRATITUDE
AIR CHIEF MARSHAL
HUGH CASWALL TREMENHEERE
DOWDING
1st BARON OF BENTLEY PRIORY
G.C.B., G.C.V.O., C.M.G.
LEADER OF 'THE FEW'
BATTLE OF BRITAIN
1940
ARCHITECT OF DELIVERANCE

Underneath the plaque, written large for all to see, is 'Born in Moffat' and then the town motto 'nunquam non paratus' — meaning Ready Aye Ready — which could hardly be more fitting. Running across the top of the wall are Winston Churchill's famous words:

NEVER IN THE FIELD OF HUMAN CONFLICT
WAS SO MUCH OWED BY SO MANY TO SO FEW

Unveiled by Muriel, the Lady Dowding, on September 9th, 1972, *above*, **the Moffat memorial to Lord Dowding was conceived by a local resident, Miss Irene Park, the daughter of a local doctor and an ex-wartime WAAF,** *below left*. **It was Miss Park's quiet but unceasing efforts from January 1971 which finally brought the impressive project to fruition. The bronze plaque, executed by Scott Sutherland and mounted in a setting designed by D. Bruce Walker, was dedicated by the Rev. Dr A. McHardy, chaplain of the Scottish Area RAFA,** *below*.

While England and Scotland have their memorials to famous Royal Air Force leaders, Wales is not without a tribute to a man of their calibre. In the village of St Clears, Dyfed, they are very proud of 'the Jones boy' one of their sons who represents thousands of his kind who were and still are the backbone of the Air Forces. His name is recorded on a stone wall beside the village war memorial in these words:

IN PROUD MEMORY OF
GROUP CAPTAIN J. IRA JONES
PER ARDUA — AD ASTRA.
BORN IN THE VILLAGE 18TH APRIL 1896. DIED 30TH
AUGUST 1960 HAVING SERVED HIS COUNTRY
FAITHFULLY AND DEFENDED IT WITH
CONSPICUOUS GALLANTRY AND DEVOTION.
THIS MEMORIAL WAS ERECTED BY PUBLIC
SUBSCRIPTION TO PERPETUATE THE MEMORY OF
A MAN OF WHOM WALES IS JUSTLY PROUD — 1964

These fine words do not reveal the great character of Ira Jones. He was a born fighter and a successful rugby player for Carmarthen Harlequins despite being only five feet five inches tall and weighing less than nine stone. He learned to shoot in the Welch Territorials, then joined the Royal Flying Corps in 1915 as a wireless operator and went to France where he pestered his superiors relentlessly until he was accepted for training as an observer.

They soon discovered what an excellent shot he was and nicknamed him 'Taffy the Tiger'. He gained the Military Medal for carrying two wounded gunners to safety and a few weeks later, like Albert Ball, he was among the British officers honoured by the Tsar of Russia with the Order of St George for their bravery. He received his observer's wing in 1916 and was recommended for a commission and pilot training in May 1917. After training at Northolt and London Colney, he was one of the nucleus of pilots who formed No. 74 Squadron.

Ira Jones had a perennial problem. While excellent in the air, his bad landings were legendary. He crashed many planes but always managed to walk away from the wreckage. It was a habit of his to offer up a short prayer of thanks every time he got back safely. In the Royal Air Force Museum at Hendon, an interplane strut from a No. 74 Squadron SE5a is on display. It is signed by Ira Jones and some of his fellow airmen.

Ira Jones was posted to France with No. 74 Squadron in March 1918. His first 'kill' was on May 8th and by Armistice Day six months later he had amassed forty victories. King George V visited the squadron in the front line in August

1918. Jones wrote in his diary, 'The greatest day of my life. I've shaken hands with my King.'

At the end of the First World War, he took over No. 74 Squadron, by then known as the Tiger Squadron and held a permanent commission until retiring in 1936. Then he took a job training pilots of the Royal Air Force Volunteer Reserve and consequently trained many of 'The Few', including 'Sailor' Malan, so called because he served several years at

The short figure of Ira Jones, commemorated in his home town of St Clears, Dyfed, in the picture *opposite*, **is seen shaking hands with King George V,** *above*, **during a visit to the Western Front in August 1918.**

sea before joining the Royal Air Force. To Ira Jones' immense satisfaction 'Sailor' led the Tiger Squadron in the Battle of Britain.

Ira Jones was recalled to service as a signals officer in 1939, but his skills as a pilot were soon put to use in forming No. 59 Operational Training Unit at Turnhouse, Edinburgh. When this was complete he moved to Heston to form No. 53

Operational Training Unit where some of the first American pilots to fly Spitfires were trained. He was a great morale booster and known to all as Grandpa Tiger although only forty-five years old. No. 74 Squadron pilots returning from a sweep over France during the Battle of Britain were not surprised to see Ira Jones get out of a Spitfire landing beside them after an unofficial flight.

11   ROYAL AIR FORCE SQUADRONS

The Royal Air Force Squadron memorials erected since the Second World War give us a fascinating glimpse of the numerous types of aircraft in service during the war, the numbers of people involved and their attitudes to the fighting.

A stranger arriving from another planet would see that Lincolnshire played a major part in the salvation of this country by the abundance of memorials there. Statues and stones vie with pillars and plaques to build a picture of the county at war.

The one at East Kirkby is outstanding. A grey pillar in memory of those who gave their lives with No. 57 and No. 630 Squadrons stands on the site of the guardroom beside the entrance to the old airfield. Both squadron badges are embossed on the pillar and above them is a picture of a Lancaster bomber in the camouflage livery which was such a familiar sight there during the latter part of the Second World War.

The pillar is flanked by two stone slabs, one with a tribute from the squadrons thanking the people of East Kirkby for their welcome during war and peace and their contribution to the memorial fund. The other is engraved with the following evocative poem by W. Scott, formerly a gunner in No. 630 Squadron:

OLD AIRFIELD
I LIE HERE, STILL BESIDE THE HILL,
ABANDONED LONG TO NATURE'S WILL,
MY BUILDINGS DOWN, MY PEOPLE GONE.
MY ONLY SOUNDS, THE WILD BIRDS' SONG.
BUT MY MIGHTY BIRDS WILL RISE NO MORE,
NO MORE I HEAR THE MERLINS' ROAR,
AND NEVER NOW MY BOSOM FEELS,
THE POUNDING OF THEIR GIANT WHEELS.
FROM THE AGELESS HILL THEIR VOICES CAST,
THUNDEROUS ECHOES OF THE PAST,
AND STILL, IN LONELY REVERIE,
THEIR GREAT DARK WINGS SWEEP DOWN TO ME.
LAUGHTER, SORROW, HOPE AND PAIN,
I SHALL NEVER KNOW THESE THINGS AGAIN,
EMOTIONS THAT I CAME TO KNOW,
OF STRANGE YOUNG MEN SO LONG AGO.
WHO KNOWS, AS EVENING SHADOWS MEET,
ARE THEY WITH ME STILL, A PHANTOM FLEET,
AND DO MY GHOSTS STILL STRIDE UNSEEN,
ACROSS MY FACE, SO WIDE AND GREEN.
AND IN THE FUTURE, SHOULD STRUCTURES TALL,
BURY ME BEYOND RECALL,
I SHALL STILL REMEMBER THEM,
MY METAL BIRDS, AND LONG-DEAD MEN.
NOW WEEDS GROW HIGH, OBSCURE THE SKY,
O REMEMBER ME, WHEN YOU PASS BY,
FOR BENEATH THIS TANGLED, LEAFY, SCREEN,
I WAS YOUR HOME, YOUR FRIEND, 'SILKSHEEN.'

A thriving aviation museum founded by the Panton brothers now stands on the old airfield at East Kirkby. One of their most recent acquisitions is the Lancaster, manufactured in April 1945 at Longbridge, which stood for many years as gate guardian at RAF Scampton. Lancasters were a common sight at East Kirkby during the war years. Of the squadrons featured on the memorial, *opposite*, No. 57 received theirs in September 1942 and No. 630 which was formed from 'B' Flight of No. 57 in November 1943 flew solely Lancasters until disbanded in July 1945. (*TF 337624*)

'Silksheen' was the radio call sign for East Kirkby — a friend indeed to those crew members in stricken aircraft returning from missions over Europe. When they heard its faint echo crackling through the ether, they knew the coast was near and they stood a chance of landing at East Kirkby. A decorative metal barrier surrounds the three stones. It incorporates the squadron numbers and a silhouette of a Lancaster bomber.

But that is not all at East Kirkby. A few years ago a local farmer Fred Panton, together with his brother Harold, bought the old control tower or watch office as the crews called it, to restore as a memorial to the fallen. They have gradually built up the Lincolnshire Aviation Heritage Centre and in 1988 acquired the Lancaster which stood at the gate of RAF Scampton. They plan to restore it in memory of their eldest brother, Flight Sergeant Christopher Panton of No. 433 Squadron who failed to return from the Nuremburg raid on March 30/31st, 1944. The Red Lion public house near the aerodrome still has a bar table upon which aircrew carved their names upon completion of thirty missions.

Also in Lincolnshire at North Killingholme, a granite pillar commemorates No. 550 Squadron. It was erected on behalf of the local people to ensure that the men of the squadron who lost their lives are not forgotten as the old airfield is redeveloped. The side of Lancaster Approach, the access road to a modern industrial site, is an appropriate setting. It was unveiled by Wing Commander Jim Bennett, DFC, who also presented a squadron badge and plaque to the parish church which reads:

PRESENTED TO THE PEOPLE OF NORTH
KILLINGHOLME BY WING COMMANDER
J. J. BENNETT D.F.C. AND BAR, FOUNDER AND
FIRST COMMANDER OF 550 (BOMBER) SQUADRON.
A TOKEN OF ESTEEM AND RECIPROCATION FOR
THE KINDNESS AND CO-OPERATION SHOWN BY
YOUR PEOPLE TO THE SQUADRON
JANUARY 1944-OCTOBER 1945

The unveiling of the North Killingholme memorial to No. 550 Squadron, *above*, and a close up of the pillar, *below*. In January 1944 No. 550 Squadron was the first to move into North Killingholme flying 'ops' over Europe, including the devastating Duisburg raid of October 1944 and their final mission on the SS barracks at Hitler's mountain retreat near Berchtesgaden.

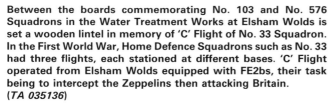

Between the boards commemorating No. 103 and No. 576 Squadrons in the Water Treatment Works at Elsham Wolds is set a wooden lintel in memory of 'C' Flight of No. 33 Squadron. In the First World War, Home Defence Squadrons such as No. 33 had three flights, each stationed at different bases. 'C' Flight operated from Elsham Wolds equipped with FE2bs, their task being to intercept the Zeppelins then attacking Britain. (*TA 035136*)

A few miles away at Elsham Wolds the water treatment works is an unusual place to find a commemorative plaque but in the entrance hall one records Elsham Wolds as a bomber station with Wellington, Halifax and Lancaster aircraft all flying on bombing missions against Germany and occupied Europe. On either side is a Roll of Honour to No. 103 and No. 576 Squadrons and a record of their honours and awards.

Outside to the left of the main entrance is a memorial garden with a damaged propeller as a centrepiece. It is from a Lancaster and commemorates all those who died while flying from the airfield. The squadron numbers are cut into the grass and filled with white pebbles, 103 on the left and 576 on the right.

In the autumn of 1989, a now-typical Lincolnshire squadron pillar joined the earlier memorials at Elsham Wolds commemorating Nos. 103 and 576 Squadrons. It stands in front of the propeller blades and displays the squadrons' badges, depicting a swan and a merlin.

A Lancaster propeller is the chief feature of the No. 9 Squadron memorial in the centre of Bardney, near Lincoln. The propeller is supported by a brick base incorporating a piece of Norwegian rock. This is from the Tromso area of Norway where No. 9 Squadron's successful attack on the German battleship *Tirpitz* took place in 1944. It commemorates men with the courage of Sergeant George Thompson, a young Scotsman who on only his fifth operation earned a posthumous Victoria Cross for rescuing the mid-upper gunner when his turret was set on fire, an exploit which resulted in both of them dying from burns. Sergeant Thompson is also commemorated by plaques in the schools he once attended in Kinross and nearby Scotlandwell.

Norway is featured again on a tall tongue of granite in Fife at RAF Leuchars — which remains an operational station — at a latitude almost as far north as Norway. The pungent smell from the local paperworks still wafts across the airfield where overshooting the runway means ending up in the stickiest mud on Scotland's coast. The pillar recalls the past with this inscription:

THIS STONE COMMEMORATES THE BROTHERHOOD
IN ARMS BETWEEN BRITISH AND NORWEGIAN
AIRMEN WHO FOUGHT FROM THESE NORTHERN
SHORES IN WORLD WAR II 1940-1945. WE HONOUR
THOSE WHO GAVE THEIR LIVES.

The memorial at Bardney to No. 9 Squadron commemorates their actions during the Second World War. These men were carrying on the traditions of one of the oldest squadrons which formed at St Omer as the first Royal Flying Corps squadron to be equipped with radio and flying BE2as. They have since flown over thirty types of aircraft from the Vickers Vimy to the Avro Vulcan and are now based in West Germany with Tornados. (*TF 120695*)

The Norwegian memorial at RAF Leuchars beside the gate guardian — a Lightning in No. 74 Squadron livery — which were flown from Leuchars between 1964 and 1967. The Norwegian links recorded on the pillar at RAF Leuchars were strong. No. 333 Squadron was formed there from Norwegian personnel in May 1943. They operated Mosquitos from the station on shipping reconnaissance along the coast of Norway and Catalinas from the nearby River Tay on patrols over the North Sea. Now No. 43 and No. 111 Squadrons are on constant alert, guarding Britain's Air Defence Region.

Leuchars also has an oak plaque in its Norman church. It is in memory of six former cadets of the St Andrews Squadron Air Training Corps who died in the war. The cadets came from St Andrews, Tayport and Newport showing what a large area of East Fife the squadron served.

Formed from Norwegian airmen who had evaded capture in 1940, No. 331 and No. 332 Squadrons arrived at North Weald with their Spitfires in mid-1942. In 1990 some of the survivors returned to lay a wreath on the Norwegian memorial, at the invitation of Epping Forest District Council. From left to right: **Brian Hudspeth (Chairman of Epping Forest District Council), ex-Lt.-Col. Ragnvald Myhre, ex-Sgt. Helge Rørvik, Lady Pike, ex-Lt.-Col. Arvid Blix, Egil Tarjusen, ex-Sgt. Inge Øvstedal and Major Hans Støvern, the Norwegian Assistant Defence Attaché.**

Further south Norway's involvement is also recorded on a rough stone column at North Weald in Essex. The inscription in Norwegian includes the dates 1940-1945 revealing that the Norwegian Air Force fought with us from the early days of the war. Following the German invasion of Norway in 1940, those airmen who escaped to Britain were quick to form a squadron within the Royal Air Force.

Two primitive figures of a man and a woman decorate the front of the column and on the back it says in English for the benefit of people like me whose knowledge of Norwegian is non-existent:

THIS MONUMENT WAS UNVEILED BY HRH PRINCESS ASTRID ON 19 JUNE 1952 ON BEHALF OF THE NORWEGIAN FIGHTER SQUADRONS WHICH SERVED AT RAF STATION NORTH WEALD DURING WORLD WAR II

It is dedicated in gratitude to the Royal Air Force, to the RAF Station North Weald and to the people of the district.

A new housing estate has now risen around the memorial in the village of Elvington to the Free French Air Force squadrons, Nos. 346 and 347, since it was erected in 1949. They returned to Bordeaux with their Halifaxes in October 1945 when they ceased to be part of the Royal Air Force. According to the plaque, in English and French, 'This monument recalls their battles and the sacrifice of their dead'. (*SE 703476*)

The Yorkshire Air Museum now stands within the perimeter of the airfield at RAF Elvington, once the home of No. 77 Squadron, where an impressive memorial has now been erected to their memory. A few yards away beside the old station chapel No. 6 Group, Royal Canadian Air Force, and No. 4 Group, Royal Air Force, are already commemorated amid carefully tended rose beds. (*SE 680482*)

More European involvement is recorded on a striking memorial to the Free French Air Force Squadrons standing on the edge of the village of Elvington, near York. The unmistakable outline of a Halifax bomber pierces an unusual stone monument which resembles a wooden vaulting horse. A column on the end has an engraved panel and beyond it a French tricolour carved in stone. On the panel in French and English it reads:

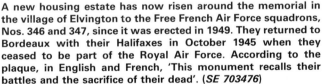

> Here was stationed Groupment de Bombardment No. 1
> comprising the French Squadrons Guyenne and Tunisie
> RAF Squadrons 346 347

The men had been transferred from North Africa in 1944 and served in Bomber Command for the rest of the war. A side view of the Halifax would show that the colours of the roundels were in the reverse order, in accordance with French national markings.

A quarter of a mile away next to the gate of the present RAF unit at Elvington but within the grounds of the Yorkshire Air Museum, a Spitfire propeller on a brick and tile base commemorates No. 4 Group of the Royal Air Force. No. 6 Group of the Royal Canadian Air Force is recorded by a plaque on the old chapel. A fine turned granite pillar forms part of a memorial to No. 77 Squadron.

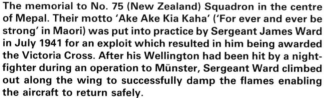

The memorial to No. 75 (New Zealand) Squadron in the centre of Mepal. Their motto 'Ake Ake Kia Kaha' ('For ever and ever be strong' in Maori) was put into practice by Sergeant James Ward in July 1941 for an exploit which resulted in him being awarded the Victoria Cross. After his Wellington had been hit by a night-fighter during an operation to Münster, Sergeant Ward climbed out along the wing to successfully damp the flames enabling the aircraft to return safely.

The memorial in Binbrook village to No. 460 Squadron, No. 1 Group's only Australian squadron. One of their Lancasters, W4783 — veteran of 90 sorties — is now on display at the Australian War Museum in Canberra. Binbrook, no longer an operational base, was the scene for a feature film remake of *The Memphis Belle* about the Eighth Air Force's first B-17 and crew to complete 25 missions. There were no less than five B-17s flying at Binbrook during filming in 1989! *(TF 210940)*

Allies from even further afield are remembered in the midst of the flat Fen country at Mepal, Cambridgeshire. Set in grass among rose beds, a modest disc rests on an octagonal base. The badge of No. 75 (New Zealand) Squadron is engraved on the top. It has a strange figure of a tiki — a Maori amulet representing an ancestor — in front of two crossed mining hammers. The New Zealand Flight who were training on Wellington bombers became No. 75 Squadron in April 1940. It was disbanded in 1945 but the squadron number was adopted by the Royal New Zealand Air Force.

Fellow Antipodeans from Australia are recorded at Binbrook, Lincolnshire on a square column with a chamfered top similar to several others in the county. It is dedicated to all those members of No. 460 Squadron of the Royal Australian Air Force who served at Breighton (Yorkshire) and Binbrook (Lincolnshire) from 1941-1945. The squadron motto was

'Strike and Return' which is appropriately illustrated by a kangaroo jumping over a boomerang on the badge.

More citizens of the Commonwealth flew from RAF Middleton St George, now Teeside Airport. Outside the airport hotel which was formerly the officers' mess is a Welsh slate memorial to three Canadian squadrons who served there. They were No. 419 (Moose), No. 420 (Snowy Owl) and No. 428 (Ghost), with their badges suitably depicting a moose, a snowy owl and a ghost. Over three hundred Canadian ex-servicemen came over for a weekend of celebrations when the stone was unveiled in 1985. A few ventured to McMullen Road, named after a Canadian Pilot Officer William McMullen who died as he steered his doomed Lancaster away from the streets of Darlington to crash in a field. His ghost is said to haunt the hangars and has been reported roaming the corridors of the former officers' mess.

Now the control tower at Wickenby hosts the budding tyros of the Robin and Cessna; then it was the pilots and crews of the Wellingtons and Lancasters of Nos. 12 and 626 Squadrons. Today the memorial to those who served, and to those who failed to return, stands beside the peri-track on the eastern boundary. (*TF 104810*)

The memorial, *above right*, at Leeds/Bradford Airport, once known as RAF Yeadon, recalls No. 609 Squadron which formed there as a day bomber unit of the Auxiliary Air Force in 1936. Redesignated a fighter unit in 1938, they took their Spitfires into the Battle of Britain and in October 1940 became the first squadron to claim its 100th enemy aircraft destroyed.

Another RAF station which is now used by civil aircraft is Wickenby, near Lincoln. At the entrance is a superb memorial to the men of bomber squadrons Nos. 12 and 626. The main feature is a magnificent sculpture of Icarus the character in Greek Mythology who fell from the skies when his waxen wings melted as he flew too near the sun. Aviation historian Alexander McKee in his book *Into the Blue* advances the theory that Icarus was not just a legend but the first man to fly. He puts forward evidence suggesting that the characters, the place of the flight and the circumstances in the legend are historical. Whatever the truth about Icarus, 'He stands for the man who flew too high, dared too much — and died.' An apt symbol for the young men who failed to return to Wickenby.

Leeds/Bradford Airport was once RAF Yeadon, the home of No. 609 (West Riding) Royal Auxiliary Air Force. They formed during the rapid expansion of the Air Force in the late thirties. Their badge is displayed in the observation lounge. Its crossed hunting horns and white rose of York above the motto 'Tally Ho' indicate that the men of the West Riding were as ready to hunt down the enemy as the House of York was during the Wars of the Roses. No. 609 Squadron was a potent factor in the Battle of Britain. One of their number, twenty-five-year-old Flight Lieutenant John Dundas is credited with shooting down the German fighter ace Major Helmut Wick on November 28th, 1940, in the process of which he lost his own life. Thousands of visitors must see this tribute every year.

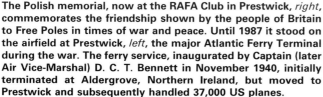

The Polish memorial, now at the RAFA Club in Prestwick, *right*, commemorates the friendship shown by the people of Britain to Free Poles in times of war and peace. Until 1987 it stood on the airfield at Prestwick, *left*, the major Atlantic Ferry Terminal during the war. The ferry service, inaugurated by Captain (later Air Vice-Marshal) D. C. T. Bennett in November 1940, initially terminated at Aldergrove, Northern Ireland, but moved to Prestwick and subsequently handled 37,000 US planes.

In stark comparison, few people could have seen the memorial to the Polish airmen at Prestwick Airport which stood neglected and damaged when I first found it on the far side of the airfield. However, it has now been fully restored and re-dedicated twice. I am indebted to Mr K. Benwell of Ayr and Prestwick Branch of the Royal Air Force Association who explained:

'The double dedication was political — the Free Poles in Scotland refused point blank to share the ceremony with representatives of the Polish People's Republic. They are truly Poles apart. On May 2nd, 1987 over one hundred members of the Polish Combatants, Polish Naval and Air Force Associations spent a memorable day in Prestwick at the headquarters of the RAFA in Ardayre Road.'

The refurbished memorial stands in the grounds surrounded by flowers in the Polish colours of red and white, against a background of blue sea and sky. The silhouette of the fine bronze eagle decorates the middle of the Polish cross on the front of the column.

The following week members of the Polish People's Republic, including General Roman Paszkowski and Polish Embassy officials from London, attended a second ceremony. The inscription on the copper plaque at the front reads:

To commemorate the friendship during the War 1939-45 and time of peace. Free Poles in Scotland, Polish Combatants, Naval and Air Force Associations.

The side panel is in Polish and translates as:
For your and our freedom — Polish Air Force.

Another damaged memorial was rescued and placed in the Newark Air Museum at Newark, Nottinghamshire. It is a simple stone commemorating No. 106 Squadron and its years of service 1917-1919 and 1938-1946. It originally served as the headstone of a mock grave at RAF Metheringham, Lincolnshire. When No. 106 Squadron was disbanded in 1946, the officers packed their hats and other souvenirs in a box with the squadron colours and buried it. Ex-Lancaster pilot of No. 106 Squadron Roy Bradley discovered the stone lying broken by the grave which had been pillaged. Only a hat band and two cartridges remained to be found and he arranged for the pieces to go to Newark Air Museum for safety. A Book of Remembrance and a memorial plaque to the squadron are in Holy Trinity Church in the village of Martin, near Metheringham.

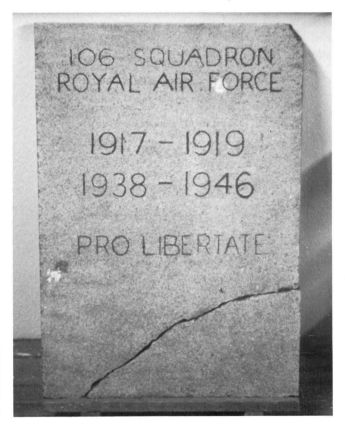

The damaged stone in memory of No. 106 Squadron in the Newark Air Museum tells only two-thirds of the story. The squadron first operated between 1917 and 1919 as a reconnaissance unit equipped with RE8s. Then from 1938 to 1946 it played its part during that war but what it does not reveal is the re-formation of the squadron at Bardney in 1959 as a Thor unit. These American ground-to-ground missiles were phased out after 1962 because they had no second strike capability and, once more, the squadron was disbanded.

The Kelstern pillar — the model for many others in Lincolnshire — was erected in October 1964, some nineteen years after No. 625 Squadron was disbanded. The red rose of Lancaster in their badge was a mark of respect for the qualities of the Lancaster — the only aircraft they flew during their two year's service. (*TF 254920*)

Still in Lincolnshire but outside again high on a windy corner of the Wolds at Kelstern stands a stone pillar in memory of No. 625 Squadron. The first one of this type in the county, it is closely resembled by those at Binbrook, East Kirkby and North Killingholme. They are solid granite and will still be standing long after all signs of the airfields have disappeared. It is sited beside the boundary of the old airfield and is well cared for by cadets of the local Air Training Corps, No. 1228 (Louth) Squadron, who form a guard of honour at the annual Remembrance Service.

At least three more memorials of this type are on Lincolnshire's soil, two erected in 1978. One at Ludford Magna, or as it was known to No. 101 Squadron 'Mudford' Magna, was dedicated in the July. It records their service in Bomber Command during the First and Second World Wars. It links up with a Roll of Honour in Ludford Magna Church, the cross at Scallows Hall described in Chapter 13 which reveals that No. 101 Squadron flew Lancasters, and a tribute in Belgium. This takes the form of a curved wall and stands on the spot at Boxbergheide in Limburg, Belgium, where three members of No. 101 Squadron, Pilot Officer John Ashton, Sergeant John Redden and Sergeant Ernest Lane, were killed when their aircraft crashed while returning from a raid on Cologne in 1941. Dedicated to all the airmen who lost their lives over the province of Limburg, it is one of many such memorials to aircrew of Bomber Command.

No. 101 Squadron arrived as RAF Ludford Magna opened in June 1943 and were there for the rest of the war flying Lancasters. Many of their aircraft carried radio counter-measures equipment operated by a German-speaking member of the crew, to attempt to confuse the enemy. On the night of June 5/6th, 1944, the jamming of enemy wireless communications was carried out by twenty-one of their Lancasters to support D-Day. The memorial is dedicated to all the airmen of the squadron who died in both World Wars. (*TF 196890*)

Members of Bravo 3 Post, Royal Observer Corps, erected the memorial to No. 100 squadron beside the Holton-le-Clay bypass as a tribute to the men of RAF Waltham for whom they had provided vital support during the Second World War. Four of the squadron's aircraft notched up over a hundred operations, 'A' Able being the top scorer with a hundred and twenty-three missions. (*TA 283030*)

A similar memorial was erected in November 1978 near Waltham, Grimsby, by the members of Bravo 3 Post — Fulstow Royal Observer Corps, to No. 100 Squadron. Their badge with its skull and crossbones symbol surmounts their motto 'Sarang Tebuan Jangan Dijolok' — Malayan meaning 'Do not attack the hornets nest'. The squadron was stationed in the Far East for eight years before reforming at Grimsby in December 1942 as a heavy bomber squadron equipped with Lancasters.

No. 170 Squadron, commemorated on the pillar at Hemswell, flew Lancasters from the station for barely a year. During that time they lost sixty-two aircrew and thirteen aircraft in more than nine hundred sorties over enemy territory. The short life of the squadron began at Weston Zoyland, Somerset, in June 1942 where, equipped with Mustangs, they took part in reconnaissance missions and defensive patrols until being disbanded in January 1944. No. 170 Squadron re-formed at Kelstern in October 1944 and disbanded again in November 1945. (*SK 947897*)

In summer 1985 yet another memorial in the same style was placed at Hemswell, near Gainsborough, to commemorate No. 170 Squadron of Bomber Command. A fine picture of a Lancaster adorns it under the motto 'To see but not be seen'. It was erected by the squadron reunion association which flourishes.

On the edge of the wartime airfield at Kings Cliffe near Peterborough is a sculpture symbolising the spirit of comradeship which existed between all Allied forces during the Second World War. Two white columns support aircraft wings carved from stone. The right hand one is the familiar elliptical shape of a Spitfire while on the left is an American Mustang. This column is engraved with the badges of the 20th Fighter Group, the 77th Fighter Squadron, the 55th Fighter Squadron, the 79th Fighter Squadron and the 97th Service Group of the United States Army Air Force. Badges of No. 616, No. 266 (Rhodesia) and No. 349 (Belgian) Squadrons of the Royal Air Force and No. 485 Squadron of the Royal New Zealand Air Force embellish the right column. Between them a black polished granite slab with gold lettering reads:

KINGS CLIFFE AIRFIELD
STATION 367
TO COMMEMORATE THE ETERNAL MEMORY OF
THOSE AMERICAN, BRITISH, BELGIAN AND
COMMONWEALTH AIRMEN WHO GAVE THEIR
LIVES IN THE CAUSE OF FREEDOM 1939-1945 LEST
WE FORGET.

The wording of the inscription on the unorthodox memorial at Kings Cliffe, near Peterborough, gives an idea of the number of different units of different nationalities which operated from the station. It was originally a Spitfire base until USAAF units arrived to train with the RAF. Thereafter it became an American base in 1943 supporting P-38 Lightnings and later P-51 Mustangs. (*TL 030983*)

Kings Cliffe reminds us of the American contribution in Britain during the war, and there is plenty of other evidence of their presence. American nationals served in the Royal Air Force and formed the Eagle Squadrons until the United States entered the war. The Eagle Squadrons became part of the United States Army Air Force in September 1942. Major General Carl Spaatz arrived in England in June 1942 and opened his headquarters in Bushy Park, Teddington

where a bronze plaque set in the American star insignia, unveiled in August 1945 commemorates all American airmen who served there. Memorials began to appear as soon as Servicemen were posted home after the surrender.

The first one to be put up in Europe was at Martlesham Heath in Essex, in memory of seventy-two airmen who died while flying from there. Captain and Mrs Eric Hervey who promoted the idea of the memorial had given up their home, Little Bealings Grove, two miles from Martlesham Heath immediately the war began. Mrs Hervey ran it as a reception centre-cum-hospital for servicemen. It was open house throughout the war with the bed patients often surrounded by visiting comrades.

Captain Hervey kept a register of all the servicemen who were listed as dead or missing. When peace came, he composed a Book of Remembrance which is now in the Library of Congress, Washington, D.C. It contains their names and addresses and all the details he knew about their last hours. Captain Hervey also sent a letter of condolence to each family and an invitation to visit Martlesham Heath. Many of them came to see the base where their sons had served and the simple memorial which records their names.

Although the memorial at Martlesham Heath records the activities of the USAAF on the station, their tenure was but a brief interlude in its long history. It first opened in 1917 when the Experimental Aircraft Flight arrived there which was joined by the Armament Experimental Flight in 1924. Testing and development continued until 1939 when the establishment moved to Boscombe Down. Soon Martlesham Heath was alive with fighters as squadrons came and went. Wartime activity reached its peak during 1943-1945.

Steeple Morden was an ex-RAF satellite aerodrome transferred to the Eighth Air Force in 1943. With bombers stationed just three miles down the road, the fighters of the 355th Fighter Group had to operate with close air traffic control with Bassingbourn during their two-year occupation, during which time they were credited with having destroyed the most enemy aircraft on the ground of any Eighth Air Force unit. In 1977 Ken Jarman, the local farmer, made the first moves to erect a memorial with the donation of a plot of land beside the old main gate. A small party of ex-355th veterans attended its dedication in May 1978 (below), the new memorial (above) being unveiled on May 12th, 1981. (*TL 302420*)

The memorial at Steeple Morden, Cambridgeshire, is simply spectacular. We were driving along the lane between Litlington and Steeple Morden surrounded by fields of barley when suddenly a high Portland stone wall was visible through a gap in the hedge. A huge four-bladed, black and yellow propeller from a Mustang, complete with spinner, nose cone and air intake is mounted against the wall as a reminder that the 355th Fighter Group was here. To the right of the propeller a Mustang is engraved above a list of the units stationed there during the war. On the left, a Thunderbolt is depicted above a summary of the missions flown from Steeple Morden. At the foot of the wall is a block of red granite inscribed with the dates of service. It looked incongruous. Then we read that it was part of the original control tower. Three old Nissen huts behind the wall remain to confirm that this flourishing farmland was once an airfield.

The characteristic style of the buildings at Bassingbourn is typical of those airfields constructed during the period when the Royal Air Force was expanded in the nineteen-thirties. When the Americans took over in 1942, they were delighted with the conditions which were luxurious compared with those airfields laid down during the war. The 91st Bombardment Group flew B-17Fs and on August 17th, 1943 led 230 machines for the raid to Schweinfurt. The memorial erected in 1978 (as depicted here) now stands against a backdrop of mature trees. (*TL 343456*)

Equally spectacular is the propeller mounted on a post within the main gate of Bassingbourn Barracks barely three miles from Steeple Morden. Once it thrust through the air on a B-17 Flying Fortress. Now it stands above a square stone base embossed with the badges of the 322nd, 323rd, 324th and 401st Squadrons of the 91st Bombardment Group which served at Bassingbourn. Unit names are engraved on a low square pillar in front of the propeller. The many vital support sections such as finance, weather and medical are recognised as well as those actively engaged in the fighting.

An individual memorial to the crew of *Old Faithful*, a B-17 Flying Fortress from Bassingbourn's 91st Bombardment Group, is at the top of the steep hill which rises through the town of Wincanton in Somerset. A flint wall on the north side of the road incorporates a plaque reading:

THIS TABLET WAS ERECTED BY THE PEOPLE OF WINCANTON IN HONOUR OF THE UNITED STATES AIRMEN WHO LOST THEIR LIVES WHEN THEIR FLYING FORTRESS 'OLD FAITHFUL' CRASHED IN FLAMES AT SNAG FARM, NEAR THIS SPOT WHEN RETURNING DISABLED FROM AN OPERATIONAL SORTIE OVER TOULOUSE, FRANCE ON 25TH JUNE 1944.

The names of the nine crew are listed below. On the opposite side of the road a public viewpoint gives a panoramic view of the Blackmore Vale. Eyewitnesses said that the crippled plane flying very low was unable to gain enough height to clear the hill and reach an airfield on the other side.

The badly-damaged Flying Fortress commemorated at Wincanton, struggling back from Toulouse with the nine young men aboard, was way off course for its base at Bassingbourn. It is believed that they had first attempted a landing at Yeovilton but were prevented from doing so by the wreckage of a crashed aircraft on the runway. They were heading for the airfield at Zeals, a few miles away, when they struck the hill.

B-17 Flying Fortress Groups proliferated in Suffolk. In Sudbury, a plaque in the Town Hall presented by the 486th Bombardment Group thanks the people of the town for their 'Fellowship, understanding and hospitality'. Another plaque in Lavenham Market Place is in remembrance of the 487th Bombardment Group 'Who sacrificed their lives in World War Two that the ideals of democracy might live'.

Both Groups were part of the 3rd Air Division of the United States Army Eighth Air Force. They used B-24 Liberators until they were re-equipped with B-17 Flying Fortresses in August 1944. After this the two Groups bombed mainly strategic targets such as factories, airfields and marshalling yards.

Another Group from the 3rd Air Division is commemorated at Mendlesham north-east of Stowmarket. A tall slender television mast stands on the disused airfield alongside the A140. The memorial is set back from the road but it is signposted and there is even a track to park on. A tablet depicting an American pilot complete with goggles is mounted on a brick wall. The inscription commemorates the 34th Bombardment Group which was the oldest Group to serve with the United States Eighth Air Force.

The Mendlesham memorial to the 34th Bomb Group, *below.*

William Dolan, right, wearing glasses, formerly the Group Combat Intelligence Officer at Grafton Underwood, after unveiling the 384th Bomb Group memorial. *Sally B*, at that time the last airworthy UK-based B-17, flies overhead. *(SP 918908)*

The United States Army Eighth Air Force was divided into three divisions. Each one had a symbol, the First a triangle, the Second a circle and the Third a square. Within the divisions each group had a letter to simplify identification in the air. Most aircraft carried a symbol enclosing a letter with its individual serial and squadron number underneath.

Many churches in East Anglia have evidence of the American 'Occupation'. Great Ashfield has a memorial to the 385th Bombardment Group and a Book of Remembrance recording over four hundred men who died while serving at the nearby base. A memorial topped by the carved head of an American airman erected in Conington churchyard near Peterborough in 1945 was replaced in 1982. Dedicated to the perpetual memory of the men of the 457th Bombardment Group who gave their lives during the war the replacement is similar to the original which had become badly eroded.

American ex-servicemen often come over to the dedication of a memorial to their old squadron. William Dolan was a pilot with the American Expeditionary Force in World War One. He served at Grafton Underwood, Northamptonshire, as Group Combat Intelligence Officer during the Second World War. He returned in 1977 aged eighty-one to unveil a solid granite monument. On one face a panel proudly proclaimed: 'The First and Last Bombs Dropped by the 8th Air Force were from aeroplanes flying from Grafton Underwood'. On the reverse side the 384th Bombardment Group were commemorated with the numbers of the Group's squadrons engraved around the base.

The memorial suffered frost damage and was replaced in 1985 by one of polished granite with the same inscription. A stained glass window in Grafton Underwood church commemorates the 384th BG. It depicts a Flying Fortress and below it are two plaques outlining the Group's history.

More veterans of the Eighth Air Force returned to RAF Ridgewell, Essex, in 1982 to see a memorial unveiled to the 381st Bombardment Group and the 432nd Air Service Group who served on the base during the war. Once again a real old timer, Lieutenant Colonel James Good Brown who was chaplain there during the Americans' tenure, performed the dedication ceremony watched by over eighty of the former servicemen. The memorial occupies part of the old hospital site. It is built of polished black granite with deeply incised gold lettering. The central panel, about eight feet high carries the triangle of the 1st Air Division. It encloses an 'L' which was the identification symbol of the 381st Bombardment Group. Underneath it and on two side wings are details of the missions flown by the 532nd, 533rd, 534th and 535th Squadrons of the Group who all operated B-17s.

In front of the panels are two granite benches. Visiting servicemen usually sit a long time reflecting on their days at Ridgewell. While other visitors find a message of hope in the inscription.

LET THIS MEMORIAL BE AN INSPIRATION TO THE OPPRESSED AND A WARNING TO WOULD-BE AGGRESSORS THAT PEACE IS OUR ULTIMATE GOAL. FURTHER, LET IT REMIND ALL FORMER MEMBERS OF THEIR PROUD HERITAGE AND GIVE THEM RENEWED STRENGTH TO MEET THE CHALLENGES OF THE FUTURE

Evergreen trees surround the memorial softening the hard lines of the granite. Behind them two dilapidated wooden huts remain of the wartime buildings.

The best place to see the symbol of the 1st Division is on the remains of the old runway at Polebrook in Northamptonshire. It is not easy to find but it is very near an aircraft hangar which is visible for miles around. A triangular slab of black granite stands as a monument to the fallen of the 351st

Ridgewell, like Grafton Underwood, has a memorial to only some of the airmen who served on the base during the war — in this case the 381st Bomb Group and the 432nd Air Service Group, USAAF. The 381st supported by the 432nd took part in nearly three hundred bombing operations including the Schweinfurt raid on which they lost eleven aircraft. The memorial is embellished by an olive branch and Indian arrows, dating back to the time when the American eagle was an Indian symbol. (*TL 747397*)

Flying Fortresses were seen at Polebrook longer than any other British airfield. The first arrived in June 1941 when No. 90 Squadron moved in with Fortress Is, the first of its type in Bomber Command. The four squadrons of the USAAF's 351st Bomb Group — the 508th, 509th, 510th and 511th — commemorated by the memorial began operations from Polebrook in April 1943. The Group's visitors during this time included Captain Clark Gable who flew five missions with them while making the training film *Combat America*. (*TL 098870*)

The EAAGA Memorials at Lippits Hill, near High Beach in Epping Forest *left* **and at Great Dunmow, just beside the Stroud Hall entrance to the airfield** *right*. **The former had a** **commemorative plaque added in May 1976 marking the 200th anniversary of American Independence, seen here being unveiled by General Ewan Rosencrans of the USAF, right.**

Bombardment Group. The inscription records the three hundred and eleven bombing missions flown from Polebrook between 1943 and 1945: one hundred and seventy-five B-17 Flying Fortresses and their crews were lost and three hundred and three enemy aircraft were destroyed.

On the matching granite plinth is an engraving of a B-17 with a triangle enclosing the letter J on the tailplane. The back of the memorial holds a surprise. A huge letter J, hundreds of times larger than the one on the plinth, almost fills the triangle leaving no doubt that the 351st Bombard-

ment Group were here. (I am reliably informed that the nearby hangar is a 'J' type but this is purely coincidental.)

Essex hosted so many American servicemen that when the war ended the Essex Anglo-American Community Goodwill Association was formed. It aimed to keep in contact with the servicemen, welcome those who returned for a visit, and erect suitable memorials. A porch and window were dedicated at Chelmsford Cathedral and stone plaques placed at Lippits Hill, Boreham and Great Dunmow which bear the triangular 1st Air Division symbol enclosing the EAAGA logo.

The 65th Fighter Wing Air Sea Rescue Control Centre was set up in the Grammar School in Saffron Walden. Reporting stations around the East Anglian coast took bearings on distress signals and relayed them to Saffron Walden. There they were plotted on two triangulation tables which covered the whole area under the Centre's control. It was also the Centre's task to co-ordinate the subsequent rescue by aircraft or, more usually, high-speed launch.

In the north-west corner of Essex at Saffron Walden, the United States Army Air Force had such a good rapport with the local people that they share a joint memorial. A well kept rose garden is the setting for a red brick wall with white panels listing the names of all the casualties. A central panel reads:

In honoured memory of the officers and men of the 65th Fighter Wing of the UNITED STATES AIR FORCE and the men and women of the BOROUGH OF SAFFRON WALDEN who gave their lives in the defence of freedom 1939-1945

The legend 'ANGLO AMERICAN MEMORIAL' is inscribed on the white canopy above the wall.

Further north in rural Norfolk a tall obelisk attracts the attention of anyone driving along the road between the A47 and Beeston. Standing in a garden beside the road it records the service of the 392nd Bombardment Group who flew Liberators from the USAAF Station 118 at Wendling.

The memorial at Rattlesden in Suffolk is very difficult to find. I drove round and round the narrow lanes early on a May morning searching for it. The mist reflecting countless fields of yellow rape transformed the whole area into a living

Two squadrons of the 322nd Bomb Group flew some of the first medium bombers — B-26 Marauders — in this country from Rattlesden before the 447th Bomb Group arrived in November 1943 with B-17s. They left Rattlesden in August 1945, their rôle now being commemorated on the airfield's memorial. (*TL 972570*)

Turner painting. It was an hour before I found it on the south side of the old airfield about a quarter of a mile from Kettle's Farm on the Brettenham Road, but worth every moment. This is the first aviation memorial that I have seen made from a Norwegian rock called Larvikite, a black stone full of sparkling blue crystals. The square symbol of the 3rd Air Division surrounding a K is engraved on the six feet high formal panel to remind us that the men of the 447th Bombardment Group were there in 1945. Flanked by two flag poles (which I have come to associate with American memorials), it contrasts sharply with the background of green trees and fields. In this quiet spot it is hard to believe that B-17 Fortresses like the one profiled on the stone used to thunder into the skies.

At Nuthampstead stands the bomber airfield constructed in Scales Park, three miles west of the A10 in Hertfordshire. During its fourteen-month stay, the 398th Bomb Group notched up nearly two hundred operations before its last mission on April 25th, 1945 when the Eighth Air Force mounted its final heavy bomber mission of the war to airfields and rail targets in southern Germany and Czechoslovakia. This magnificent memorial was built by the 398th Bomb Group (Heavy) Memorial Association under the auspices of the Nuthampstead Airfield Research Society and unveiled in 1983. (*TL 413344*)

Plenty of signs of an airfield remain at Goxhill in the north of Lincolnshire although it has reverted to farmland. The USAAF Fighter Training Group formerly based there is commemorated by a single propeller blade from a P-38 Lockheed Lightning mounted on a York stone base. Erected by the local people and their friends, many of whom remember the Americans' presence, it was unveiled in 1984 by three ex-servicemen of the USAAF. The inscription below two hands clasped in greeting is simply 'Gone, but not forgotten'.

The day I visited the old USAAF base at Nuthampstead in rural north-east Hertfordshire a large party of visitors was expected. Temporary signs throughout the small village pointed to the sites of the officers' mess, the main gate, the guardroom and various other parts of the wartime airfield. It was hard to picture the huge complex that had existed in this quiet corner. A long belt of trees known as 'Flying Fortress Belt' was planted alongside the old runway and is now quite mature, but the runway itself was dug up and used as foundations for the M1 motorway. Nuthampstead was also short listed at one time for the site of London's third airport but eventually escaped such a fate.

An official memorial stands opposite the Woodman Public House. Again it is to a Bombardment Group, this time the

398th (Heavy) Bomb Group and is one of the most imaginative designs I have seen. A vertical slab of black granite has a superbly detailed engraving of a B-17 Flying Fortress on it. The flat surfaces are polished and the engraved ones unpolished and barely recognisable as the same stone. The careful shading gives the whole aircraft a lifelike appearance of roundness. The back has a plan view of the airfield in the same style. On the white marble plinth is a gold badge of the 398th Bombardment Group (Heavy). In the Woodman, which once echoed to the sounds of American voices, hangs a picture of the airfield during the war and other memorabilia of those days.

A few miles away over the Cambridgeshire border at Duxford are more reminders of the USAAF, but this time a Fighter Group. Just inside the main gate an engraved stone records details of the 78th Group's combat missions from the

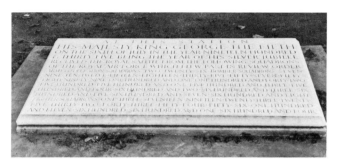

base between 1943-1945. They destroyed over six hundred enemy aircraft during this time. The stone is a tribute to their courage and the devotion to duty of all ground staff. It was taken to RAF Lakenheath when the airfield closed but was returned in 1976 when Duxford Aircraft Museum opened and is now surrounded by aircraft of every description. Some of the aircraft in the collection are themselves memorials, for example a Mustang in the 78th Fighter Group colours.

Duxford has a second valued memorial which is sited alongside the first one. It is a raised horizontal slab of stone

engraved with the following words showing that Duxford was not only an American base.

AT THIS STATION
HIS MAJESTY KING GEORGE THE FIFTH ON THE SIXTH OF JULY IN THE YEAR NINETEEN HUNDRED AND THIRTY FIVE BEING THE YEAR OF HIS SILVER JUBILEE RECEIVED THE ROYAL SALUTE FROM THE FOLLOWING SQUADRONS OF THE ROYAL AIR FORCE WHICH FLEW PAST IN REVIEW ORDER. ARMY CO-OPERATION SQUADRONS TWO. TWENTY-SIX. BOMBER SQUADRONS SEVEN. NINE. TEN. TWELVE. FIFTEEN. EIGHTEEN. THIRTY-FIVE. FIFTY-SEVEN. FIFTY-EIGHT. NINETY-NINE. ONE HUNDRED AND ONE. ONE HUNDRED AND FORTY-TWO. FIVE HUNDRED. FIVE HUNDRED AND ONE. FIVE HUNDRED AND THREE. FIVE HUNDRED AND FOUR. SIX HUNDRED AND TWO. SIX HUNDRED AND THREE. SIX HUNDRED AND FIVE. SIX HUNDRED AND SEVEN. SIX HUNDRED AND EIGHT. FIGHTER SQUADRONS ONE. THREE. SEVENTEEN. NINETEEN. TWENTY-THREE. TWENTY-FIVE. THIRTY-TWO. FORTY-THREE. FIFTY-FOUR. FIFTY-SIX. ONE HUNDRED AND ELEVEN. SIX HUNDRED. SIX HUNDRED AND ONE. SIX HUNDRED AND FOUR.

The King reviewed all three services in his Jubilee year. At Duxford he wore the uniform of a Marshal of the Royal Air Force and was accompanied by the Queen, the Prince of Wales, the Duke and Duchess of York and Lord Trenchard. The review was not a performance of aerobatics and speed which was characteristic of contemporary flying pageants at Hendon but a formal flypast of all the squadrons present. Then No. 19 Squadron who were based at Duxford thrilled the crowd with a display of squadron drill in their Gloster Gauntlets.

The service of dedication of the memorial plaque (on left of picture) in the Kirk of St Kilda was conducted by the Reverend John Barry, who was instrumental in its erection, in May 1979. Present at the ceremony were relatives of some of the airmen who lost their lives on the islands.

13   THE LAST DITCH

Crash site commemorations can hardly be regarded as aviation achievements but they are 'landmarks' and they do show the types of aircraft flying, especially during the Second World War, and the countries and people affected by it. The mountainous areas took a heavy toll as bad weather conditions hid their treacherous heights. Sites in Scotland reveal that the whole of Great Britain was involved in the fighting, not just those airfields in close proximity to Europe. Even remote St Kilda rising 1,300 feet from the Atlantic Ocean and over one hundred miles from the Scottish mainland was scarred by war. A plaque in the church on Hirta — the largest island of the St Kilda group — records that a Sunderland, a Wellington and a Beaufighter all crashed into the islands.

The most inaccessible site is surely the one marked by a cairn and a huge cross on Ben More Assynt, West Sutherland. It is a memorial to the crew of an Anson which crashed there in 1941. A commendable series of events began when a passing hill walker saw a plaque among the ruins of a cairn on a plateau below the summit of Ben More Assynt. He piled up the stones and propped up the plaque, noticing that it was to six members of an Anson crew. He mentioned it to an

acquaintance back in Aberdeen who happened to be the Commanding Officer of No. 2489 (Bridge of Don) Air Training Corps Squadron. Later when the Commanding Officer, Flight Lieutenant Niall Aslen, was describing the rôle of the RAF Mountain Rescue Service, he told the cadets about the Anson crash. They soon decided that they would like to build a proper memorial cairn as a mark of respect.

Flight Lieutenant Aslen, an experienced mountaineer, explained how difficult the conditions were in the area but the cadets, always ready for a challenge were not deterred. They designed a cairn, researched the history of the Anson and organised the expedition. The ill-fated aircraft was from No. 19 Operational Training Unit on a flight from RAF Kinloss when it ran into a snow storm over Stornaway. Turning at Cape Wrath they tried to climb above the bad weather but the last thing that was heard was a faint morse message saying 'icing up . . . lost power in port engine . . . losing height . . . descending through 3,000 feet.' The pilot Flying Officer James Steyn D.F.C. attempted a forced landing on the high plateau but unfortunately the plane hit a knoll and broke up.

The pilot, navigator and wireless operator were killed instantly. The three trainees in the rear survived briefly then succumbed to the cold icy conditions. The bodies which were not found until five weeks later were buried at the spot owing to the difficulties of getting them down the mountainside.

Owing to the remote nature of the demise of Avro Anson N9857 of No. 19 OTU, on Ben More Assynt in Sutherland, Scotland, the bodies of the crew were buried on the site and the grave marked with a cairn, which by August 1984 had badly deteriorated, *above left*. In June 1985 the cairn was re-built and re-dedicated in a ceremony attended by relatives of the crew in June 1985 *left*. The crew are also remembered on a memorial in Inchnadamph Old Churchyard, the nearest village, *above*.

Forty-four years later in May 1985, ten cadets and their two leaders spent a week erecting the new cairn which is topped with an eight-foot cross. From their base camp at Inchnadamph they carried thirty-pound packs of cement on their backs for five and a half miles to the scene of the crash, and gathered eleven tons of limestone blocks for the cairn. Once again the weather was bad. They were unable to complete the cairn but the plaque was polished with the sort of effort they normally reserved for the toes of their boots and placed ready for a memorial service on the final day. The short service attended by relatives of the crew provided a fitting climax to the cadets' efforts and they returned home full of plans to go back and complete it. Bad weather during their second expedition caused them to revise their plans for restoring the whole site.

They left the cairn in a watertight state to prevent it from shattering in the winter when the temperature dips as low as minus twenty degrees centigrade. The snow covers the top of the cross in winter and its weight can move almost anything. One of the Anson's engines has been carried two hundred metres downhill. Few people spot the cross from the ground but appropriately Royal Air Force crews see it during training flights over Scotland because its whiteness stands out against the grey green of the mountainside.

The death of the Duke of Kent, the first son of an English sovereign to be killed on active service for more than 500 years, received scant coverage in newspapers of the time, with the result that this incident, which claimed the lives of fourteen men, is relatively unknown. The rear gunner, Sergeant Andrew

Jack, survived, albeit badly burned and injured. This 'then and now' view shows the site before being totally cleared and today, with the memorial cross, bearing the names of all those killed, standing on the site. Nothing of the Sunderland remains on the hillside.

A more modest plaque commemorates the crew of another Anson of No. 19 OTU who struck Ben Macdui, almost the highest point of the Cairngorms in August 1942. A little more altitude and they would have cleared the top.

Much closer to civilisation, the Cheetah engine from an Anson was set on a concrete base outside Loch Thom Forestry Centre, south of Greenock, in 1976 by the Scotland West Aircraft Investigation Group. The aircraft crashed into Dunrod Hill near the loch in July 1939. It was from No. 269 Squadron who were based at Abbotsinch (now Glasgow Airport) on coastal reconnaissance duties.

War casualties affected families at all levels of society. The Duke of Kent, father of the present Duke, was killed when a Sunderland flying boat of No. 228 Squadron which he was travelling in crashed in the far north of Scotland near Berriedale in August 1942. The aircraft was on its way to Iceland when it hit a hillside scattering wreckage over a wide area before catching fire. The only survivor of the crew of fifteen wandered off and was found hours later in a dazed

condition. The Duke had been a keen flyer and the first member of the Royal Family to fly across the Atlantic. A monument marks the point of the impact.

Still in Scotland, at Gatehouse of Fleet a granite block with a brass plate stands in memory of the Canadian pilot of a Typhoon from No. 440 Squadron who crashed in 1944. The aircraft's propeller boss was cemented into it but has become badly corroded. Pieces of the plane were scattered around the site up to the seventies when even the wing markings were still discernible.

Not all crashes were due to warfare. Two in the fifties involved Vampires from Fleet Air Arm Squadrons. A cairn and memorial cross on the desolate mountainside of Ben Klibreck, Sutherland, commemorates the crew of one from No. 736 Squadron which crashed there in 1955. Another crashed at Rawmarsh, near Rotherham in 1959. The pilot was a midshipman, Ian Wilson. His body was never recovered so the ground was subsequently consecrated and guarded by railings.

The memorial erected in June 1955 by Horwich Rotary Club stands near the spot where the Wellington captained by Australian Flight Sergeant J. B. Timperon crashed on Angle-zarke Moor in November 1943. It was built in a more accessible position for the benefit of visitors, near the footpath once trodden by the lead miners as they made their way up to Lead Mines Clough. From the bottom of the valley it stands on the skyline as a permanent reminder of the supreme sacrifice paid by just one crew. (*SD 629165*)

Nothing guards the pillar which the Rotary Club of Horwich, Lancashire erected in memory of the crew of a Wellington that crashed on the moors. 'The Bomber Memorial', as it is known locally, stands high above the town commanding a spectacular view of the surrounding countryside. The club members visit the site regularly to keep it in good order and hold an annual service of remembrance.

In 1981 the newly formed Machynlleth Aircraft Discoverers group restored a plaque at Pennal in the Dovey Valley commemorating the crew of a Wellington which flew into the mountainside in bad weather.

Although the high ground took its toll of aircraft, many met their end in lowland areas often due to enemy action. Lancaster crash sites are legion, showing what a large rôle this admirable aircraft fulfilled.

The marble cross in the woodland near Scallows Hall, Lincolnshire is typical. It gives the names of the crew of a No. 101 Squadron Lancaster which crashed in December 1943. In

A plain cross at Scallows Hall, near Binbrook, marks the spot where a Lancaster crashed killing seven members of the crew. The plane, a Mk III, DV270, was from No. 101 Squadron operating from Ludford Magna. (*TA 247948*)

Lancaster ED503 from No. 9 Squadron stationed at Waddington ended its days twenty miles away in a field near Sibsey on January 29th, 1943. The families of the five airmen killed — Donald Brown, Charles Cocks, John Doran, Thomas Henry and Bobby Lind — joined together to erect the monument to their memory north of Sibsey. (*TF 334535*)

New pupils at All Saints School on the outskirts of Leicester receive instant lessons in drawing, engineering and history when they see the huge picture of Lancaster, PA269, in the corridor. The six Polish airmen of No. 300 Squadron commemorated on the plaque there survived the loss of their own country and fought throughout the war only to lose their lives when their aircraft, based at Faldingworth, Lincolnshire, crashed on the site of the school in 1946.

Lincolnshire earlier the same year a Lancaster of No. 9 Squadron had crashed in the middle of the flat fen north of the village of Sibsey. You can imagine the feelings of the families as they unveiled an unpretentious cross as a tribute to their sons. It remains in the centre of a vast field unseen from the road and reached only with difficulty across a ploughed field.

In contrast, hundreds of pupils see the plaque in the corridor of All Saints School, Wigston. It records the crash of a Lancaster on the school's site in February 1946. The six names of the Polish crew who died are given but they are overshadowed by an eight feet high cutaway diagram of a Lancaster showing full details of the airframe and engines.

Our allies in the Royal Canadian Air Force are remembered for an exceptionally gallant deed at Wallingford, Oxfordshire. In September 1944 a Halifax of No. 426 Squadron took off from RAF Benson with a full bomb load. As the pilot Flying Officer John Wilding cleared the runway he realised that the aircraft was in severe trouble. Knowing that he was heading straight for Wallingford, he instructed the crew to bale out and steered the now blazing plane away from the town. It crashed in a field and exploded killing Flying Officer Wilding and the flight engineer, Sergeant Frank Andrew, who had remained at his post. The people of Wallingford recognised their courage by erecting a pillar of

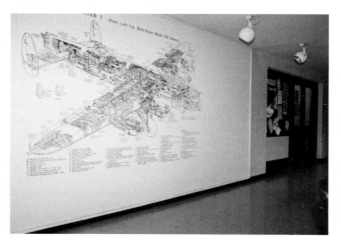

The crew of the Halifax commemorated at Wallingford took off from RAF Benson on September 9th, 1944 on a bombing operation although the station is better known for its wartime photo-reconnaissance rôle. Then the Mosquito was most commonly used, but Spitfires, Blenheims, Wellingtons and Ansons also played their part. Today Benson is the home of the Queen's Flight which includes Andovers, Wessex helicopters and, more recently, BAe 146 jet airliners.

Cotswold stone at the junction of Wilding Road and Andrew Road on a new estate with a plaque explaining how the roads got their names. The pillar has a No. 426 Squadron badge on it with ironically the squadron motto 'On Wings Of Fire'.

Despite the many types of aircraft already mentioned, many more became familiar sights in the skies of Britain when the United States of America entered the war, as we can see from many of the plaques, pillars and posts around us. Bombers and fighters alike are commemorated. Different nationalities of men and machines are recorded nationwide, in some cases together.

At Somerleyton, Suffolk a stone records the death of an American crew in a British Mosquito. This classic aircraft, powered by two Rolls-Royce Merlin engines, was versatile enough to be used in the rôles of bomber, day and night fighter and reconnaissance plane. It was also used as a strike aircraft against enemy shipping with tremendous effect. The one at Somerleyton flown by the two Americans took off from Coltishall. They dealt with an enemy bomber then went after a V1 flying bomb, determined to destroy it. They crossed into the anti-aircraft zone and the gunners thinking it was an enemy plane fired at it. The two crewmen tried to fire the colour of the day with their Very pistol to show that they were friendly but it jammed and tragically they were brought down.

One unlucky American crew of a Martin Marauder are listed on a memorial in a lay-by in the Llanberis Pass in North Wales. They were on a routine ferry flight to Lancashire from Florida via Brazil, Dakar and St Mawgan and were on the short last leg of the journey expecting to land in an hour and a half. However, strong winds blew them off course and they hit the side of Y Garn just north of Snowdon.

In 1975 Arthur Evans and his fellow enthusiasts of the Snowdonia Aviation Group set up the plaque at the foot of the mountain. 'I thought our wartime allies deserved a small memorial,' he explained. 'It was very different from one we were involved with at Penmaenmawr,' he went on. 'Then we had a Jolly Green Giant to lift the memorial up the mountain to the place where the Liberator crashed.'

'The mountain' was Moelfre and 'The Liberator' — named *Batchelor's Baby* — had left RAF Valley on Anglesey on

The memorial erected in 1980 to five of the men aboard American Liberator *Batchelor's Baby* and their mascot Booster who died when the aircraft crashed high in the Welsh mountains during a transit flight in bad weather. Now all the airmen who lost their lives on the mountains in the Second World War are commemorated by the cross placed there by the Snowdonia Aviation Group.

January 7th, 1944 in poor visibility. The pilot, Major Adrian Schultz, was supposed to follow another aircraft but could not see it in the snow-filled clouds. He clipped a wing on a peak and had no alternative but to attempt to land his crippled craft on the mountain. Major Schultz and five of the crew survived while a passenger, four crewmen and their mascot dog, Booster, perished.

The 'Jolly Green Giant' was a Sikorsky HH53 of the United States Air Rescue Recovery attached to RAF Woodbridge, Suffolk. The memorial — appropriately Welsh slate from a quarry in Llanberis — was installed together with a cross to all Allied airmen who died on the mountains. Arthur Evans and his stalwarts erected the stone and joined Major Schultz and a small party who braved the weather on the snow-covered slopes for a short dedication service.

Bad weather over Exmoor caused another American Liberator to strike Hurlstone Point and crash on the marshes at Porlock in September 1942. An unusual plinth shaped like cog wheels supports a small memorial to the crew. It takes twenty minutes hard walking along the beach from Porlock Weir to reach the spot on the edge of the marshes where it stands battered by storm and sea.

A mystery surrounds a third Liberator which crashed near Cheshunt, Hertfordshire in 1944. A plaque which used to hang in Cheshunt library has the following message:

The shape of the memorial at Porlock is reminiscent of the front half of a Vulcan fuselage, but in fact it commemorates an American Liberator. Eight airmen died when one crashed on the marshes behind the stone.

TO THESE GALLANT AMERICAN AIRMEN
WHO ON AUGUST 12 1944, SACRIFICED THEIR
LIVES TO PREVENT THEIR AIRCRAFT FROM
CRASHING ON OUR HOMES.
THE RESIDENTS OF CHESHUNT AND WALTHAM CROSS
IN THE COUNTY OF HERTFORDSHIRE
DEDICATE THIS PLAQUE IN
GRATEFUL MEMORY.
2nd LT. JOHN D. ELLIS 2nd LT. ROBERT B. COX
S/SGT. JAY V. CABLE
T/SGT. STANLEY F. JANKOWSKI
S/SGT. CLARE W. HULTENGREN
T/SGT JOHN H. HOLLING
F/O SAMUEL D. STALSBY
S/SGT. WILLIAM C. McGINLEY
S/SGT. FRANK MINICK S/SGT. JACK O. SHAEFFER
577 BMB. SQ. 392 BMB. GP. USAAF

I was puzzled by the name Clare on the crew list but am reliably informed that it is occasionally used as a man's name in the United States. The local people collected so much money in gratitude to this brave crew for avoiding their homes that the surplus was sent to Freckleton, near Preston to help rebuild a school which had just been destroyed by another Liberator. The plaque has since been moved to the American Cemetery at Madingley.

Historian Peter Rooke in his book *Enfield at War* writes that the story was wishful thinking by a *News of the World* reporter as witnesses of the crash said that the tail of the bomber was missing which would have made it impossible to steer. However, he agrees that keeping the memory of the crew alive is the important thing.

No doubts surround the heroic action of Lieutenant Arthur Brown who was killed at Nantwich, Cheshire. He stayed with his plane to make sure it missed the town. The tale is told in simple words on a stone which marks the place of impact:

HERE LIES 1st LIEUTENANT
ARTHUR L. BROWN
U.S.A.A.F.
AGED 23 YEARS
OF NEW YORK
WHO CRASHED
IN HIS THUNDERBOLT
TO AVOID THIS TOWN
JAN. 14th 1944

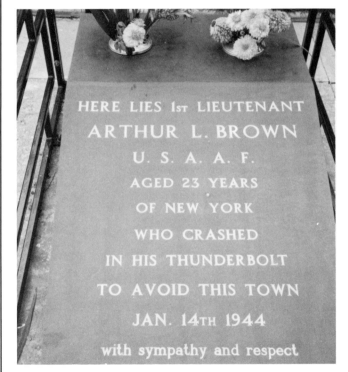

The grave of 1st Lieutenant Arthur Brown lies beside a popular public walk near the point where the railway crosses the River Weaver and can be reached from an opening in Shrewbridge Road opposite Brookfield Park.

Although some human remains were recovered from the crash site and buried in the American Cemetery at Madingley, Lieutenant Brown's mother remained firmly convinced that her son lies beneath the memorial, and who are we to dispute a mother's intuition? Mrs Gladys Henshall of Nantwich has put fresh flowers at the spot every month for over forty years and kept in touch with Lieutenant Brown's family. His sister, also named Gladys, came over to England in 1985 to meet Mrs Henshall.

Not all American aircraft crashes were confined to the war era. A small tablet in a field at Carsphairn near Loch Doon records the loss of the crew of a Boeing Superfortress in July 1951. The aircraft was a tanker on a routine navigation training flight from Lakenheath to Prestwick. *The Times* reported an eye witness as saying that 'It was making an unusual noise and appeared to get into difficulties, flying around in circles then smoke appeared. It crashed exploding immediately and bursting into flames.' All eleven members of the crew on board were lost.

These are just a few of the memorials to crashes in this country. There are many more and plenty of evidence of aircraft types. Dozens of wrecks in various stages of recognition lie on the hillsides of the Peak District, Wales and Scotland. Societies are devoted to the recovery of wreckage and the marking of the appropriate locations. Scotland has nearly four thousand known crash sites. Flight Lieutenant Aslen formerly of Bridge of Don Air Training Corps knows of one hundred and nineteen Whitley sites alone. Many unofficial memorials exist such as one at Glen Affric in the Highlands where an engine and propeller have been cemented into a wall by a bridge. Forestry workers often find wreckage and prop some of it up to mark the spot.

The Dumfries and Galloway Aviation Group placed a memorial stone on the summit of Cairnsmore of Fleet in 1980 aided by a Sikorsky helicopter of the USAF. (The word 'Army' was dropped from the USAAF in 1947 after the National Security Act established the United States Air Force by combining the Army Air Force, Army Air Corps and Air Force Combat Command.) The stone bears the names of all the airmen they could trace who had crashed to their deaths in the Galloway Hills.

Further south in the deceptively tranquil Clee Hills is a unique memorial embracing the twenty-three Allied and German victims of crashes on the hills between 1939-1945. Phillipa Hodgkiss of the Marches Aviation Society cast an eagle from metal recovered from each of the crash sites, now mounted on the memorial stone which is dedicated to friend and foe alike.

A stained glass window holds one of the earliest clues to flying in Britain. In Malmesbury Abbey, Wiltshire, in a window at the western end of the south aisle, is the figure of Elmer with a pair of wings strapped to his chest. He was an 11th century monk who was regarded as an expert on science. He took a great interest in the sky and saw Halley's Comet twice. His ambition was to fly. After constructing a pair of wings he tied them on and launched himself from the Abbey's tower. His 'flight' lasted about two hundred yards before he crashed to the ground breaking both legs. He attributed his failure to lack of a tail which was probably close to the truth but the Abbot banned any further attempts so Elmer had no chance to prove his theory.

Nine centuries later the rapid development of aviation is depicted in a window installed in the Church of St Columba at Kinloss on the coast of the Moray Firth in Scotland. It commemorates the 65th anniversary of No. 120 Squadron. At the top are the graceful lines of a DH9 which was the first aeroplane the squadron used in 1918. The upper wing of the biplane stands proud on its struts above the open cockpit, the blunt nosed fuselage and the fixed undercarriage. It was built to carry out bombing raids on Germany and over three thousand had been produced by the end of the war.

No. 120 Squadron was disbanded in 1919 but it re-formed as a maritime reconnaissance squadron in 1941. In the centre of the window the squadron badge features an Icelandic Falcon, reflecting the time the squadron was based in Reykjavik between 1942-1944. No. 120's main task was U-Boat patrols to protect shipping bringing vital supplies from North America. At the bottom of the window is the squadron's present aircraft, a Nimrod, the upswept tail and refuelling probe contrast sharply with its predecessor as it flies over the grey-green wastes of the Atlantic Ocean.

Much further south, seven biplanes fly over the smooth green of the Lincolnshire countryside in a three light window at St Mary's Church, Welton. The centre light is occupied by St Michael piercing a dragon with a picture of Lincoln Cathedral underneath. The two side lights are full of soaring planes seen from every angle. Camels, Blackburns and Avros circle above an old canvas hangar. The window was unveiled in 1920 by the Vicar of Welton, Canon A. Hunt, who was the Padre at nearby Scampton during the Great War. The design must have been very modern for its era. It commemorates the officers and men of the Royal Flying Corps and the Royal Air Force who died for their country.

The aircraft depicted at Welton are those flown from RAF Scampton — then known as Brattleby — during the First World War, and contrast strongly with the Red Arrows' Hawks and the aircraft of the Central Flying School. (*TF 012798*)

lined helmets worn by pilots to keep out the cold. The main figure above the airfield is of St Michael, and below it the legend:

TO THE GLORIOUS MEMORY OF
MAJOR LANOE GEORGE HAWKER VC, DSO, RFC.
30th Dec 1890-23rd Nov 1916

Major Hawker won the first Victoria Cross to be awarded for aerial combat in July 1915. Flying a Bristol Scout of No. 6 Squadron, he attacked three enemy aircraft, damaging two and destroying the third.

The window was designed by Francis Skeat of my home town of Harpenden in Hertfordshire. He also had the pleasant task of designing a window for Valley Church, Anglesey (depicted below), which was to be a gift from the

Major Hawker successfully led No. 24 Squadron of the Royal Flying Corps on operations from Bertangles, just north of Amiens. Their DH2s brought down many German aircraft, but Major Hawker finally became the eleventh victim of Manfred von Richthofen: 'The Red Baron'.

An airfield complete with hangars and aircraft shines out from a window of Longparish Church, Andover. It depicts Bertangles in France which was used by the Royal Flying Corps during the First World War. The scene is flanked by two sentinel figures in the heavy leather overcoats and fur-

The great window at Rolls-Royce, Derby, commemorating the close association between the company and the Royal Air Force. Rolls-Royce have built engines for the RAF right from the early days of the First World War when they produced the Eagles and Falcons; through the Second World War with the legendary Merlin and into the jet age with the Derwent.

servicemen of RAF Valley to the local people in appreciation of the kindness shown to all ranks during their long association. The window has Christ as the central figure standing on a circle of stars above the following words:

This window is the gift of the officers: warrant officers: non commissioned officers and airmen of the Royal Air Force Valley.

On either side of it is a kneeling figure of an airman in modern flying kit.

Strangely enough some of the most magnificent windows also emanated from Harpenden. The designs of Hugh Easton for Rolls-Royce, the Royal Air Force Chapel in Westminster Abbey and the St George's Chapel at Biggin Hill were all made up in a small glazier's shop in Harpenden. Hugh Easton's most spectacular work must surely be the window in the front hall of the Rolls-Royce factory at Derby.

The central figure is a fighter pilot of the Royal Air Force ready for action in his flying suit and Mae West with his helmet in his hands. He stands on the spinner of a Merlin propeller with its three blades stretched out over the rooftops and smoking chimneys of the Derby factory which produced the engines. Above the pilot's head is a huge golden eagle and behind it, filling the top of the window, is a blazing sun.

The whole idea of this window was to have a lasting record of the close association between Rolls-Royce and the Services. Their most famous engine was the Merlin, used during the Second World War to power Spitfires, Mosquitos, Hurricanes and Lancasters as well as many other aircraft. Its most vital rôle was during the Battle of Britain which is the theme Hugh Easton used when designing the window. His idea was to symbolise the work of men's hands in the lower part of the window as the body. The pilot represents the brain and the eagle the heart and the spirit. While the sun in all its glory stands for the ideals for which the Battle of Britain was fought. The inscription below the propeller reads:

THIS WINDOW COMMEMORATES
THE PILOTS OF THE ROYAL AIR FORCE WHO, IN
THE BATTLE OF BRITAIN TURNED THE WORK OF
OUR HANDS INTO THE SALVATION OF OUR
COUNTRY.

The day of the unveiling, January 11th, 1949, is long remembered in Derby. A special train brought Royal Air Force personnel and other guests from London to join members of Rolls-Royce company for the celebration of their joint efforts. Lord Tedder, Marshal of the Royal Air Force and deputy Supreme Commander of all Allied Forces under General Eisenhower at the time of the Second Front, and Viscount Trenchard headed the guests at the luncheon table. Lord Dowding was present and Group Captain Douglas Bader was among the many Battle of Britain pilots in attendance. Not so easily recognised but equally deserving of a place was Sydney Camm, designer of the Hurricane. Lord Tedder unveiled the window, then after a service of dedication, groups of guests toured the works. The day shift employees finished one hour early to enable them to see the window while the night shift viewed it the following morning. Then, thousands of Derby's citizens accepted the invitation to see it during the following weeks.

Most windows of this magnitude are in churches or cathedrals. Surrounded by the many airfields of East Anglia, Ely Cathedral has a Royal Air Force window dedicated to the members of No. 2, No. 3, No. 8 and No. 100 Groups who served in the district during the Second World War.

No. 2 Group was made up of light bomber squadrons flying aircraft such as Blenheims, Bostons and later Mosquitos. No. 3 Group comprised heavy bomber squadrons with Stirlings and Lancasters. No. 8 Group, better known as Pathfinder Group, had their headquarters at nearby Huntingdon, while No. 100 Group were a Bomber Support Group with a special rôle. Their task was to wage war against enemy communications and so lessen the enormous losses encountered by Bomber Command. They jammed enemy radar by dropping 'window' (strips of metallic foil) and using spoofing devices. Later in the conflict they flew Mosquitos as escorts for bomber streams, attacking German night fighters. The cathedral window includes two pictures of men in uniform and badges and scenes of the Groups' activities.

Lincoln Cathedral, the landmark for so many pilots returning to bases in Lincolnshire, has the Airman's Chapel of St Michael (the traditional Christian helper against evil). There are four windows. One depicting a New Zealand pilot and another in memory of Rhodesian airmen. The third is dedicated to Bomber Command officers and other ranks, while the fourth is to Flying Training Command. This one has a picture of the Royal Air Force College at Cranwell and a minute aircraft. Some of this glass was also made in Harpenden to the designs of Christopher Webb, a St Albans artist.

Another window in Lincolnshire is in the parish church at Croxton, commemorating Sergeant T. I. Dee, RAF VR. (The VR after his name indicates that he was a volunteer reservist.) His brother John Dee, one of the present

The window at Ropsley is unusual in including a photographic likeness of William Dale, aged twenty-two, whom it commemorates and was his family's personal tribute. He is portrayed standing, wearing flying clothing with his dog at his side. (SK 993343)

churchwardens at Croxton, told me that the family decided on a traditional window but that there is a Lancaster on the headstone of Sergeant Dee's grave a few feet from the porch.

Also in Lincolnshire is my favourite window. It is in Ropsley Church and depicts the figure of an airman wearing a parachute and a Mae West yet neither saved the life of William Philip Dale whom it commemorates. He was lost during an operation over Ostend in November 1941. To me it is the faithful dog at his feet in the manner of a knight of old that is so touching.

Many airmen were shot down over the sea and saved by the rescue services. In St Mary's Church, Dover, is a window dedicated 'In memory of all ranks of the Allied Air Forces and Air-Sea Rescue and Marine Craft sections of the Royal Air Force who perished in the seas throughout the world during the Second World War.' The window shows the sea with the white cliffs of Dover in the background. A Walrus flying boat is airborne above an air-sea rescue launch; both are racing towards an airman in an inflatable dinghy.

The sea is also featured in the Coastal Command Commemorative Window at RAF Northwood, which remains the headquarters although it is now part of Strike Command. The picture is full of detail. The central feature is a figure in aircrew flying kit complete with helmet, goggles and Mae West, operating an Aldis signalling lamp. He is standing on a pile of weapons, including a depth charge, a torpedo and a bomb, which were all used against enemy shipping. A Sunderland flying boat, backbone of the Royal Air Force's maritime war effort is flying in from the left. On the right is a Shackleton which replaced it in 1951. Below seven different types of ships on the blue and white sea are under heavy attack. Above the main figure are the ensigns of the Royal Navy and the Royal Air Force and the badge of Coastal Command. Its motto 'Constant Endeavour' echoes the long hours of routine patrols when crews might be in the air for periods up to twelve hours. It stretches across the bottom of the window between the Red and Blue Ensigns which are a reminder of the part played by the Royal Fleet Auxiliary, the Merchant Navy and the fishing fleets.

This window was planned by Air Vice-Marshal C. E. Chilton CB, CBE, and the detailed design work carried out by a National Serviceman, Norman Attwood, while both were on the staff at Coastal Command Headquarters.

Not all windows are in memory of Service personnel. In the isolated parish church at Glenapp, between Stranraer and Girvan, is one in memory of the Hon. Elsie Mackay, daughter of the Earl of Inchcape. She died while attempting to cross the Atlantic with Captain W. R. Hinchcliffe from east to west in 1928. They took off from Cranwell in a Stinson monoplane and were never seen again. She would have been the first woman to fly the Atlantic and it would have been the first east-west crossing by an aeroplane.

In her capacity as Lord Warden of the Cinque Ports, Queen Elizabeth The Queen Mother unveiled the memorial window in the Church of St Mary the Virgin, Dover, in 1980 dedicated to members of the Allied Air Forces, and the Air-Sea Rescue and Marine Craft sections of the RAF.

The Coastal Command commemorative window at RAF Northwood *opposite* includes almost every aspect of its activities. Northwood is now the headquarters of No. 18 Group formerly Coastal Command until it was absorbed by Strike Command in 1969.

COASTAL COMMAND

CONSTANT·ENDEAVOUR

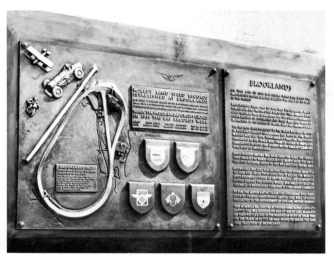

15   ONCE AN AIRFIELD . . .

Hundreds of disused airfields exist but Brooklands in Surrey is one of the best known. Its fame as a motor racing circuit is recorded on a huge memorial wall with the inscription 'BROOKLANDS 1907-1939' standing out in large letters. The chequered pattern of the winner's flag decorates one end. Beside the lettering is a bronze plaque with a plan of the circuit and a short history of Brooklands. A small biplane left of the circuit diagram is the clue to the aviation connection.

Hopeful aviators began to occupy the centre of the motor racing circuit soon after it was completed, the idea being to attract crowds to the motor racing. Moore-Brabazon, Alliott Verdon Roe, the Short brothers, Tom Sopwith and the Vickers Company were among the early tenants. Roe made the first unofficial flight in England there in 1908. The *Daily Mail* Round Britain Air Race in 1911 put Brooklands firmly on the flying map.

Vickers started a flying school there in 1912 training many men who became First World War flying aces. During the war the Vickers factory expanded rapidly producing over four thousand aircraft mainly the FB (Fighting Biplane) series. The Vimy bomber was developed too late to take a significant part in the war but it achieved fame when Alcock and Brown used it for the first transatlantic crossing in 1919.

In spite of the success of his triplanes at Brooklands, and the thousands of Avro 504s built during the First World War, Alliott Verdon-Roe sold his share in Avro in 1928. He then joined S. E. Saunders of Cowes to form Saunders-Roe where he indulged in his greatest interest of developing flying boats.

After the Armistice, Brooklands evolved as a focal point for light aircraft. The first post war flying school opened, operated by Colonel C. L. P. Henderson, who designed and built several of the aircraft. One of them the Gadfly, broke the world's height record for light aircraft in May 1929.

The Brooklands Aero Club formed in 1930 offered flying training and courses in aero engineering. A year later the College of Aeronautical Engineering was established there. The thirties-style clubhouse is now listed as a building of historic interest. As the threat of another war loomed over Europe, flying took on a more serious aspect and the Hawker Hurricane made its first flight at Brooklands in 1935.

Motor racing ended in 1939 but flying continued. The Wellington designed by Barnes Wallis of 'Dambusters' fame also made its first flight there and over two thousand five hundred more were built by Vickers.

After the Second World War Vickers, by then Vickers Armstrong, bought Brooklands. They laid a new runway and expanded their works. The Vickers Viscount, the first turboprop airliner in the world to operate on a scheduled service, soared into the skies above Brooklands in the fifties.

The last aircraft to be produced there was the Vickers VC10 civil airliner, the final one taking off in 1970 after which the runway was closed.

Today there is an ever-growing collection of aircraft and other memorabilia at Brooklands, and plans for new exhibitions in the near future.

The huge memorial unveiled by Lord Brabazon in 1957 is imposing but does not diminish another unique one also at Brooklands. Few men unveil their own memorial but in 1954 A. V. Roe did just that. He uncovered a stone pillar with a plaque bearing these words:

A. V. ROE
FROM this area, on various dates in 1907-8, A. V. ROE made a series of towing flights and flight trials with an aircraft of his own design and construction, powered in the later trials by an 18/24 h.p. Antoinette engine.
THESE trials were made along the finishing straight of the motor-racing track, on this site.
A. V. ROE thus became the first of the long line of famous pioneers and pilots of many nations who made air history on this flying field of Brooklands.
THIS tablet was placed here in June 1954 by VICKERS-ARMSTRONG Aircraft Division and was unveiled by Sir ALLIOTT VERDON-ROE
then in his 78th year.

A less well known landmark recording the activities of A. V. Roe is a plaque fixed to the Victorian railway arches at Hackney Marshes. His prized Bullseye triplane was assembled there during a period when he was not welcome at

Brooklands because he had crashed a previous aircraft on the motor racing circuit. His brother used the trademark 'Bullseye' for the braces he made in a factory near the family home in Manchester, and Alliott Roe used it in recognition of his brother's financial and moral support.

Like Bert Hinkler he was also inspired by watching birds fly. An albatross followed his ship when he sailed from South America to England during his days in the Merchant Navy, prompting him to start experimenting with paper planes much to the amusement of his shipmates. Immediately he reached home in Manchester he expanded his activities to include wooden models which he flew from the roof of the house. In 1907 he won £75 in a *Daily Mail* model aircraft competition at Alexandra Palace in north London and used the money to set up at Brooklands where he built a full-sized version of his model biplane.

On July 5th, 1983, Air Chief Marshal Sir Harry Broadhurst, a former Station Commander, unveiled the memorial at Hornchurch which commemorates all aircrew and ground personnel who served there between 1928 and 1962. Hornchurch was a Sector Station in No. 11 Group and in the forefront of the Battle of Britain.

A few miles east of Hackney Marshes stands the stone monument dedicated to all personnel who served at RAF Hornchurch, but it only tells half the story. It was certainly RAF Hornchurch from 1928 until it closed in 1962 but prior to that it was known as Sutton's Farm. Lieutenant Leefe Robinson took off from there on the memorable night when he destroyed the first Zeppelin over England and earned himself a Victoria Cross. My husband Cliff has a particular interest in this airfield because a BE2c from his old squadron, No. 13, was the first plane to land there.

Sutton's Farm was one of the nine sites chosen as Air Stations to defend London from German airship raids. Two BE2c single-seater fighters were stationed there to bring the Zeppelins down. It was a David and Goliath situation but the little planes — almost twice as fast as the Zeppelins — were able to out-manoeuvre the giant airships and attack their vulnerable undersides. Fire was an airship's chief hazard because the gas bags were filled with highly inflammable hydrogen. Once it caught alight the huge craft was doomed.

Another famous aviator to fly from Sutton's Farm was Captain Tryggve Gran, the Norwegian of Cruden Bay fame. He flew BE12s for the Royal Flying Corps in an attempt to fight off German Gothas in 1917. After the Armistice the airfield returned to farmland and once again the cattle were able to graze undisturbed.

Sutton's Farm re-opened as RAF Hornchurch in 1928. Station strength built up gradually until three squadrons of Spitfires were at readiness when war was declared in 1939. The Hornchurch Wing played a vital part in the evacuation of Dunkirk, gaining four Distinguished Flying Crosses and a Distinguished Service Order during the struggle. This was followed by their even more distinguished involvement in the Battle of Britain.

Statistics do not reveal the superhuman efforts of those who flew endless sorties against the enemy, or of those ground crews at Hornchurch who serviced and refuelled the planes while bombs were falling around them. The station remained in the front line throughout the war. Whereas Hitler's bombs failed to defeat it, London's post-war urban growth succeeded, and Hornchurch closed in 1962.

Amid the urban sprawl to the west of London at Hounslow lies Heathrow, the world's busiest international airport. It completely overshadows the former airport at Hounslow only a mile and a half away. Along the Staines Road a plaque by the entrance gate to the remains of Hounslow Heath records Hounslow as being the first civil airport in the country but its

life was short. Civilian pilots used it until the Royal Flying Corps took it over in 1914 for training purposes.

After the First World War ended it reverted to civilian use. It was the only aerodrome near London with customs facilities. Hounslow was the take-off point for the first scheduled London-Paris flight in August 1919. The aircraft was a converted de Havilland bomber. Four passengers crowded warm and dry in the small cabin while the pilot was at the mercy of the weather in an open cockpit. When the Army reclaimed the land in 1920, the flights transferred to Croydon and the airfield closed.

Hendon was known originally as London Aerodrome. The name of the man who made it famous — Claude Grahame-White — is wrought in iron in the old gates beside the entrance to the RAF Museum. He made the first night flight in an attempt to gain a £10,000 prize for a non-stop London to Manchester flight. A Frenchman, Louis Paulhan, won the prize but Grahame-White took the glory for his nocturnal efforts. He opened at the airfield, put up a factory and started a flying school where Mick Mannock, Albert Ball and Reginald Warneford were among his pupils. During the First World War Grahame-White manufactured thousands of aircraft while alongside him the Royal Naval Air Service used Hendon as a training station.

After the war extravagant flying displays were staged by the Royal Air Force to increase its popularity. They grew more elaborate every year and attracted up to two hundred thousand spectators. Hendon rivalled Ascot and Henley as a social occasion. It can also boast four more 'firsts': the first aerial post in 1911, the first commercial passenger flight of twenty minutes with nine passengers in 1913, the first King's Cup Air Race in 1921 and the first flight of a British monarch to the capital in 1936.

The Royal Air Force took over Hendon in 1927. Auxiliary Squadrons No. 600 (City of London) and No. 601 (County of London) moved in and were soon joined by No. 604 (County of Middlesex). Their flying displays ended in 1937 for safety reasons because housing estates were nudging the edge of the airfield. During the Second World War Fighter Command flew from Hendon but gradually support units moved in.

In post-war years increased development around the airfield forced flying to stop. In 1972 the Royal Air Force Museum opened on the site, joined later by the Battle of Britain Hall and the Bomber Command Museum, both now merged with the main museum. The Royal Air Force station finally closed in April 1987 when the remaining support and trooping units moved to RAF Stanbridge.

The first municipal airport at Bristol was four miles along the road to Wells at Whitchurch where as a small child I lived for a short time during the Second World War. I still have hazy memories of a huge hangar with a gloomy interior, and what seemed very large aeroplanes with sloping backs showing green and brown patches. A housing estate now covers the airfield with the roads named after aircraft.

Much sharper memories come flooding back of a white stone column standing outside the gates of HMS *Sultan* at Gosport, Hampshire as a reminder of the naval airfield known as HMS *Siskin* which closed in 1956. The inscription commemorates the long association between Gosport Airfield and the development of aviation in the Royal Navy and the Royal Air Force. The Gosport tube which enabled a pilot to communicate with his crew was developed at and named after the airfield. All the world's famous airlines used it for over thirty years.

On top of the column is a fine golden eagle with outspread wings which I remember well. It was a sunny Sunday afternoon when Cliff and I with our daughter Clare pulled up outside the guardroom of HMS *Sultan* to take a photograph of the memorial. Cliff got out of the car and approached the guardroom where we could see four young naval ratings behind the glass. He introduced himself, explained that he was making a photographic collection of memorials and asked if he could take a picture. The ratings exchanged significant glances, then one stepped forward. He was not exactly fat. There was just too much flesh around his ready smile.

'Just a minute,' he said. 'I'll get the broom.'

'What do you need a broom for?' Cliff queried as he disappeared into the guardroom.

'We've got to turn it round,' said number two. 'It's facing the wrong way.'

Number one rating reappeared brandishing the guardroom broom.

'What do mean the wrong way?'

'Well, we get fed up with looking at him so we turn him round for a change,' said number one, aiming the broom at the bird and missing in his anxiety to avoid trampling on the surrounding flowerbeds and so incurring the wrath of his superiors. He tried again and succeeded in getting the reluctant bird to move slightly.

'He's supposed to face sou'sou'west,' he said giving it another whack.

'It's all right where it is,' protested Cliff. I think he feared for the gold paint.

'It's no trouble,' replied the holder of a second broom who had joined us. 'Won't take a minute.'

The conversation continued along these lines. The young men obviously regarded someone who went around photographing memorials for a hobby as a welcome diversion. A third broom appeared wielded by a thin gangling youth determined to join in the fun, while the fourth rating was draped over the side of the car talking to Clare. I sank down in my seat to watch the fun. The bird was now in a perpetual

The development work mentioned in the inscription on the memorial to HMS *Siskin* — Gosport airfield — refers mainly to the work on torpedoes which began at RAF Gosport during 1914-1918. The torpedo unit remained after RAF Gosport was handed over to the Fleet Air Arm in 1945 when the airfield was renamed HMS *Siskin*. Navy helicopters operated from the airfield for ten years but the torpedo unit was the last to leave when it transferred to RAF Culdrose in 1956 when the airfield closed.

spin as blows rained down on it from all sides. Cliff was almost in orbit as he raced about trying to get a front view of the bird, but he couldn't hold his camera still for laughing. It was twenty minutes before we finally drove away with the broom platoon hastily reshuffled to form a guard of honour, brooms held at present arms to mark our departure as number four finally peeled himself off the car.

These cheery young men must be the eighties version of those who frequented Tarrant Rushton just a few miles across the Dorsetshire border. A variety of units operated from there and are recorded on a stone memorial with a very comprehensive copper plaque.

A plan of the original airfield shows the three intersecting runways flanked by the station buildings. A picture of Pegasus in the right hand corner is an apt symbol for the Airborne Division of the Army. Aircraft of No. 38 Group took off from there with the 5th Parachute Brigade during the D-Day landings. Above Pegasus is the badge of the United States Airborne Army Division who also operated from Tarrant Rushton. In the centre is the Royal Air Force Crest and below it the initials S.O.E. of the Special Operations Executive. The Flight Refuelling Company logo is on the left. It was founded at nearby Wimborne by Sir Alan Cobham of flying circus fame. The Lancaster PA474 is linked with Flight Refuelling because it was in service there before becoming part of the Battle of Britain Memorial Flight. The legend simply commemorates 'All who operated from Tarrant Rushton between 1943 and 1980,' when it closed.

The S.O.E. also operated from Tangmere, near Chichester, about sixty miles due east of Tarrant Rushton. The airfield is commemorated by a plain stone in the village stating that Tangmere was famous in two world wars and in the forefront of the Battle of Britain.

In the Tangmere Military Aviation Museum nearby, memorabilia of No. 43 Squadron and No. 1 Squadron which spent many years there jostles with a Spitfire simulator. The late Jim Beedle, ex-No. 43 Squadron and author of its history *The Fighting Cocks*, was a co-founder of the museum. His idea was to have a constantly changing display which was made possible by the continuous flow of items arriving from ex-squadron members and others.

One of the prize exhibits is the tattered uniform of Wing Commander James Nicolson, the only Fighter Command pilot to be awarded a Victoria Cross during the war.

Wing Commander Nicolson's own memorial is not far away at Southampton, on Millbrook Industrial Estate where a

The copper plaque at Tarrant Rushton illustrates the many activities which went on at the airfield. The 'FR' logo represents the work of Sir Alan Cobham who founded Flight Refuelling Limited at nearby Wimborne. An ex-RFC pilot and aerial adventurer, he pioneered in-flight refuelling during the 1930s and re-established the company in 1948.

The plaque marking the spot where Wing Commander Nicolson touched down after baling out is now surrounded by factory units. He survived his burns and returned to operations only to die in a Liberator crash in the Bay of Bengal in 1945. The memorial was unveiled by his widow Muriel on August 16th, 1970 — the 30th anniversary of his VC exploit.

copper plaque, similar to the one at Tarrant Rushton, mounted on a stone column, bears the following words:

> On or near this spot on the 16th August 1940 during the Battle of Britain the late Wing Commander (then Flight Lieutenant) J. B. Nicolson V.C. D.F.C. R.A.F. of No. 249 Squadron, landed after parachuting from his burning Hurricane following an engagement with the enemy. After being hit and his aircraft set on fire, he continued with the action and was successful in destroying an Me 110 before abandoning his aircraft. For this act of gallantry he was awarded the Victoria Cross, the only pilot of Fighter Command to be so honoured during World War II.

Above the wording is an engraving of a Hurricane and the badge of No. 249 Squadron.

Another Southampton story is linked to Castle Bromwich in Birmingham. The Spitfire, designed and developed at Supermarine in Southampton, was produced in a huge factory alongside Castle Bromwich airfield to supply the Royal Air Force's needs. Over eleven thousand Spitfires were made

Castle Bromwich — inseparable from the Nuffield factory alongside — saw the birth of eleven thousand Spitfires and three hundred Lancasters which were test-flown from here. Now all has gone under the sprawling Castle Vale housing estate. As the memorial, originally erected in 1965, was constantly being vandalised, *top*, it was removed to the safety of the grounds of St Cuthbert's Church and rededicated on September 10th, 1988 *above*.

there. Castle Bromwich had seen many types of aircraft since the first one landed there in 1909. The Royal Flying Corps was there during the First World War then between the wars it became a civil aerodrome. The King's Cup Air Race drew huge crowds to Castle Bromwich which was a staging post and the strangely named Railway Air Services made increasing use of it.

A Royal Auxiliary Air Force Squadron, No. 605 (County of Warwick) was formed there in 1926. During the 1940s Spitfires dominated the scene. Various ground units also operated from there. Looking at the high rise flats covering the area now it is hard to believe that aircraft ever flew there. For many years a concrete pillar with a large bronze badge contradicted this impression. It stood in the middle of Castle Vale Housing Estate with a plaque reading:

> This badge was erected over the entrance to the officers' mess at RAF Station Castle Bromwich in 1938. The badge was removed to its present site by Birmingham City Council in 1965 in recognition of the long association between the City, the Royal Flying Corps and the Royal Air Force at Castle Bromwich.

It was unveiled by Mr Alex Henshaw, Chief Test Pilot at Castle Bromwich during World War II, on October 9th, 1965.

Unfortunately the memorial suffered from constant vandalism and was rebuilt on a new site in 1988. It now stands within the grounds of St Cuthbert's Church, Tangmere Drive.

Alex Henshaw, an experienced aviator of the thirties, made international news when he won the Britannia Trophy in 1939 for flying a specially adapted Percival Mew Gull to South Africa and back in four days and ten hours. As chief test pilot at Castle Bromwich, his workload was punishing. He made over six thousand test flights in Spitfires.

Still in the Midlands, at Perton on the outskirts of Wolverhampton, a six-ton boulder — an unusual choice for a memorial but not unique — rests in the middle of a shopping precinct as a reminder that this was once an RAF station.

Another boulder marks the derelict airfield at Yelverton, Devon, which was RAF Harrowbeer for just four years. The boulder had lain on Roborough Down for a hundred and fifty years after falling off a tramway wagon while being taken to Plymouth to build the harbour. This time an RAF Sea King helicopter lifted it onto a lorry as part of a training exercise, after which it was taken to Tavistock to be engraved.

RAF Harrowbeer had a brief but busy life. Thirty-four units were stationed there at different times, using over a dozen different types of aircraft. The Air-Sea Rescue Service operated from the base as well as fighters, bombers and

The memorial boulder among the new houses behind Sainsbury's at Perton is unusual in that is is dedicated to all members of the Royal Air Force — not just those who operated from the airfield. It was erected in 1982 by Wolverhampton and District Royal Air Force Association and stands on the site of the former main runway.

training units. Airmen from Canada, Czechoslovakia, Rhodesia, the United States and Poland served there alongside those from Britain. No. 302 'Poznan' Squadron was the first one to arrive with Spitfires in October 1941. A short history of the station is written on the boulder which commemorates all those who served at Harrowbeer. The first Station Commander, Group Captain Edward Ward, unveiled it in 1981, those present included Antoni Wronka, ex-No. 302 Squadron, who travelled from Warsaw for the ceremony.

Poland was one of the destinations of the 'Moon Squadrons' from Tempsford, located where the River Ivel meets the Great Ouse in Bedfordshire. The old airfield known as Gibraltar Farm was camouflaged to look like a farm, with crops flourishing alongside the brown and green painted runways. Looking down on it now from the hill at Everton all is calm and peaceful. Just off a Roman road where Caesar's legions marched so long ago, an ancient barn stands isolated in the middle of a field. A faded windsock flutters near it. The Special Operations Executive (S.O.E.) operated from here, with Nissen huts nestling within the farm buildings, and it is appropriate that a commemorative plaque is mounted in the old barn. Inside its massive timbers bare red brick walls reach the roof and concrete shelves where supplies were stored line each side.

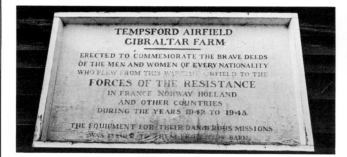

Several visitors to the old barn at Gibraltar Farm have reported feeling a shudder as though an aircraft was landing outside. Others have felt a sudden drop in temperature, often associated with the presence of a ghost but, true to its secretive wartime rôle, Gibraltar Farm's mystery remains unsolved. The plaque, which commemorates the brave deeds of the men and women who flew from there to Occupied Europe, was originally fixed on the outside of the barn but was restored and moved inside when the building was repaired in 1987. Note the altered style of lettering! (*TL 193525*)

Tempsford came to life on moonlit nights when the men of the S.O.E. took to the air. They dropped arms, agents and supplies to the Resistance forces in occupied territories, flying such aircraft as Whitleys, Halifaxes and Stirlings. The smaller Lysanders landed behind enemy lines to deliver and pick up agents. They often operated from airfields nearer their destinations such as Tangmere.

The Special Operations Executive were not forgotten when French museum authorities set up a display depicting the Battle of the Plateau des Glieres a few miles south of Geneva. Over two hundred members of the Resistance lived rough on this high plateau and were sustained by the S.O.E. until they were eliminated by the Germans. In the museum a plaque lists six members of the crew of a Halifax from No. 138 Squadron who were killed when it crashed after being badly damaged by gunfire in August 1943 while dropping supplies.

Roy Buckingham, formerly a Warrant Officer who served at Tempsford, remembers his time there as the most significant period of his life.

'I've never felt so alone,' he recalled. 'It was so different from flying with the Main Force. You had to be so accurate. It was like delivering a package to someone's back garden. We were called the 'Moon' squadrons because we only flew on moonlight lights. It was map reading all the way from the coast at low level. We flew to France, Denmark, Norway, Poland, wherever we were needed,' he went on. 'It was highly individual work. One of my friends opened the hatch in readiness one night and his two Norwegian passengers jumped out straight away several miles short of their target. A month later they came back to Tempsford. He thought they'd be after him and kept out of the way but they found him. He was very relieved when they shook his hand and one said, "You dropped us very nicely thank you but it was a very long walk".'

Tempsford was the home of two RAF Special Duties squadrons, No. 138 and No. 161, both of which arrived in March and April of 1942 respectively. By July of 1943 the Polish personnel at Tempsford were numerous enough to be gathered together as one unit — No. 301 Polish Flight. Between April 1942 and May 1945 these three units delivered some 29,000 containers (each holding 220lbs of stores), 10,000 packages and 1,000 agents to Occupied Europe. The barn at 'Gibraltar Farm' on Tempsford aerodrome was used to store the equipment and parachutes used by the SOE agents — in recent years the barn has been restored and the wooden memorial plaque moved inside the building — it is just visible through the doorway.

FURTHER AFIELD

Although this book is chiefly concerned with landmarks in Great Britain, I have already touched on a few overseas. Early flights across water such as Bleriot's over the English Channel and the R34 airship across the Atlantic were invariably marked at both ends. A few of them, however, must suffice as representative of the hundreds around the world.

The most significant, and also one of the largest, records the first flight of the Wright brothers in North Carolina. A colossal grey granite monument stands twenty metres high on top of Kill Devil Hill, a huge dune dominating the sandbanks at Kittyhawk where the brothers carried out their experiments. They chose the area because they judged the wind conditions and large sandy stretches between the dunes to be suitable for gliding. Their first motorised flight was not so much a beginning but an end to a long series of experiments with gliders and kites.

They were building and repairing cycles when the trials carried out by pioneer aviator Otto Lilienthal with gliders attracted their attention. They read all available material about flight, covering both the habits of birds and the theories and experiments of would-be aeronauts. As a result they decided to build a large kite in 1899 to try out their own ideas. Next they constructed a glider and tested it at Kittyhawk. It made record glides but these were not fully controlled. The brothers suspected that published figures of lift and resistance of wings were wrong. Orville then built a wind tunnel and tested over two hundred curved and flat wing surfaces. Then, like the monk Elmer over eight centuries before, they decided that the tail was the vital factor. As soon as they added one which could be moved, their glider became fully controllable. At last they were ready to add an engine and take to the air.

The Wright brothers had always had a flair for inventions. Their mother was a great influence in their lives. Money was short and if she wanted something she made it. When he was

Where it all started — the memorial site at Kittyhawk where the Wright Brothers first flew, seen here after the unveiling.

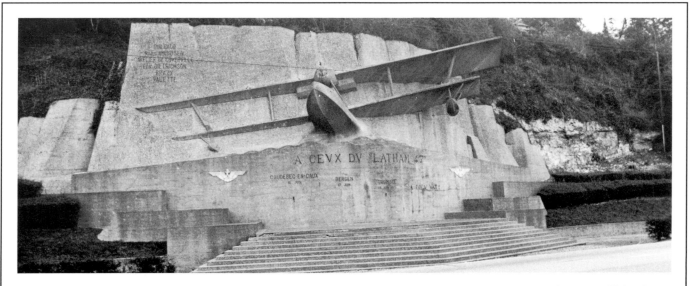

The Latham 47 immortalised at Caudebec-en-Caux was the second of the two prototypes which were built, the first one having been destroyed by fire. Only twelve production models were made before the company was taken over. Flying boats were produced there for many years — the old factory is still there, although engaged on different products today!

in his 'teens Wilbur invented a simple machine for folding newspapers to take the boredom out of one of his part-time jobs. Between them the brothers printed handbills and rebuilt bicycles; anything to earn a few dollars. Their bicycle business became so successful that they had to move to larger premises three times in the first year.

At Kittyhawk replicas of the workshop and shed used by the brothers contrast sharply with the smart Visitors' Center. Inside, the museum area displays the story of flight but naturally concentrates on the achievements of Orville and Wilbur Wright. The monument is a triangular shaped column with the names 'WILBUR WRIGHT AND ORVILLE WRIGHT' truly 'writ large'. In Statue of Liberty style it has a staircase inside leading to an observation platform at the top.

A boulder inscribed with the following words marks the exact place where the first flight began.

THE FIRST SUCCESSFUL FLIGHT OF AN AIRPLANE
WAS MADE FROM THIS SPOT BY ORVILLE WRIGHT
DECEMBER 17th 1903 IN A MACHINE DESIGNED AND
BUILT BY WILBUR WRIGHT AND ORVILLE
WRIGHT.

THIS TABLET WAS ERECTED BY THE NATIONAL
AERONAUTICAL ASSOCIATION OF THE USA
DECEMBER 12 1928. TO COMMEMORATE THE
TWENTY-FIFTH ANNIVERSARY OF THIS EVENT.

A stone slab marks the spot where Orville Wright landed, recording the distance and time — 120 feet and 12 seconds — and the date. Three others mark the length of successive flights made that day, the longest nearly a minute.

The most incredible aviation memorial in France is at Caudebec-en-Caux on the north bank of the River Seine. The river is wide here. Huge oil tankers on their way upstream to Rouen glide past a full size concrete replica of the Latham 47 flying boat which surges theatrically from the wooded cliffs above the place where it was built and launched. It commemorates the first and only voyage of the ill-fated craft.

The Latham 47, one of two prototypes, was among the aircraft which joined the search for Umberto Nobile and the crew of the Italia airship which had crashed on the ice east of Spitzbergen after flying over the North Pole during a scientific expedition. Explorer Roald Amundsen who had been on a previous expedition with Nobile asked the French

Government to help him look for the survivors after a faint radio message was heard on June 3rd, 1928. They sent the Latham 47, commanded by Captain Guilbaud and it took off from Caudebec on June 16th, 1928. The first stop was Bergen where Amundsen and a Norwegian pilot, Lief Dietrichsen, embarked. The next stop was in the far north at Tromsøe where final preparations were made for the search. They left on June 18th but were never seen again.

The Italia expedition became notorious for the number of lives lost in the rescue attempt. Twenty-two aircraft, two dog teams and fifteen ships manned by over fifteen hundred men from eight nations joined in the search. The death toll among them was horrific, while nine of the eighteen men aboard the Italia survived.

In a comparatively short time since its birth, aviation was caught up in war. The enthusiastic pilots began to fall in battle. The era of the flying 'Aces' dawned as numerous individual memorials to men of many nationalities shows.

American involvement is recorded at Luxeuil-les-Bains near Basel. A plaque was unveiled to l'Escadrille Lafayette (Corps d'Aviation) after the First World War. It was composed of American volunteers who formed a unit within the French Air Service, beginning as Escadrille Americane, but the German government objected so it was changed to Escadrille Lafayette. In February 1918 it became the 103rd Aero Squadron of the United States Air Service.

Eighty miles north-west of Basel wings of a different kind are immortalised at Fort de Vaux where the last pigeon to fly out of the fortress during the Battle of Verdun in 1916 was awarded the Croix de Guerre. The story is recorded on a plaque which also commemorates all pigeon fanciers who lost their lives in the war.

Sadly, the aviation landmarks in France are almost exclusively concerned with warfare. Day trippers from Dover can see a stark skeletal belfry at Audinghen near Calais. The belfry belonging to the new church of St Pierre supports three bells from the original church and resembles the shape of a Spitfire wing as a tribute to the Royal Air Force.

At Lorris, deep in the Forest of Orleans stands a memorial to the Resistance forces. Known as the Maquis, they had been very active here and on the receiving end of many supply drops by the Special Operations Executive. They also helped Allied airmen avoid capture by putting them in touch with the people who ran the escape lines down to Spain. The monument is a long stone wall bearing the names of members of the Resistance. Dominating the names is the date August 14th, 1944 — the day that the Germans wiped out the encampment killing over sixty of the Maquis. Crosses stand

The wing-shaped memorial belfry at Audinghen — destroyed in 1944 — was built in honour of the forces which liberated France.

among the trees where the victims fell. A row of forty-seven shows where others were forced to dig their own graves before being shot.

Not far away is a memorial to the Canadian crew of a Lancaster which crashed in fog while dropping supplies to the Resistance in June 1944. The names of the crew of eight are listed on a white stone column surrounded by an iron fence. The gate is flanked by two propeller blades from the crashed plane.

Hudson IIIA, serial FK803, was shot down by a German night fighter over Huperdange, six kilometres north of Clervaux — the ultimate destination for the three Belgian Secret Service agents was the German town of Erfurt — they never arrived.

However, a happier event is marked in the Forest of Fréteval, west of Orleans. As the war drew to a close, it was increasingly difficult to send Allied airmen down the normal escape lines and instead they were concealed in camps in remote areas. At Fréteval a tall wing-shaped monument marks the spot where a hundred and fifty two Allied airmen were liberated on August 13th, 1944 by no less a person than Airey Neave who had already escaped from Colditz castle, and a group of Special Air Service men.

Further north, in the Ardennes above the Belgian town of Spa, another wing shaped column commemorates the crew of a Lancaster which crashed on St George's Day in 1944. It came from No. 550 Squadron at Waltham, Grimsby, and was the only Lancaster lost out of the eighteen from the Squadron when it took part in a raid on Dusseldorf.

Also in the Ardennes but this time in Luxembourg, the wreckage of a Hudson from No. 161 Squadron based at Tempsford lies around six graves high on the hillside above Maulusmillen. The aircraft was N for Nan which set off to drop three Belgian agents, in March 1945. The agents and three of the crew died when the plane crashed near its destination. The villagers buried them all at the site. When peace came the War Graves Commission wanted to exhume the bodies and re-inter them in the official cemetery at Hotton in Belgium. But the villagers insisted on keeping 'our young men' — the relatives of the Allied airmen (two British and one New Zealander) gave their consent, so the authorities settled for erecting symbolic headstones, bearing the inscription 'to the memory of' and 'Buried in Maulusmillen in Luxembourg', at Hotton instead.

The Airborne Memorial at Heelsum is almost entirely built from battlefield debris of Operation Market Garden — the archway is constructed of supply canisters welded together and the fence posts are artillery shell-cases, all framing an anti-tank gun.

The Netherlands also hosts many landmarks from the Second World War. At Heelsum, near Arnhem, a superb memorial to the Airborne Troops stands in a garden, with the unmistakable figure of Pegasus — symbol of the airborne troops — and the figure of a man hanging from a parachute silhouetted against the wide Dutch sky. They are supported by a beam on two cross poles which frame a field gun.

Further north, Norway has plenty of evidence of the many British planes which came to her aid when she was invaded by German troops and during the subsequent occupation. We have our son, Nevil, to thank for the picture of the memorial in Bodo, taken while on detachment there with Treble One Squadron. Bodo was the scene of outstanding courage shown by three young airmen during the fight to stop the German troops capturing Norway. In Rensåsen Park two columns of grey granite have raised black lettering on them. 'Gloster Gladiator' can be picked out of the Norwegian inscription under the names of Flight Lieutenant C. B. Hull, RAF, Pilot Officer J. Falkson, RAF, and Lieutenant A. Lydekker, RN. The trio survived the battle of Bodo but all died later in the war.

In May 1940 these three pilots of No. 263 Squadron volunteered to provide air support from a temporary airstrip made of wooden planks at Bodo to prevent enemy troops

The local people of Bodo built the wooden runway used by the three British Sevicemen commemorated on the memorial, but it has long been replaced by a modern airfield shared by military and civil operators. No. 332 Squadron of the Royal Norwegian Air Force uses an underground hangar gouged out of solid rock for their F-16s of the Quick Reaction Alert Force.

from reaching Narvik. For a period of two days they caused mayhem among the German aircraft in their Gladiators and enabled two thousand British and Norwegian troops to be evacuated from the Rognan area. They destroyed several enemy planes and continued to fight until their aircraft were put out of action. In between fights they helped to repair the runway so that they could take off again without getting bogged down in the mud.

The Lancaster which crashed at Michelbach took off from Scampton on January 28th, 1945 for a raid on Stuttgart. Karl Frauhammer, the Hungarian refugee who built the memorial, fought on the Russian front with the German Army and was badly injured and invalided out. His gesture was entirely for peace and his thoughts only with the relatives of the seven young men of No. 153 Squadron who died: **Flying Officer Owen Jones, the pilot, Sergeants John Dormer, John Milburn, James Coles, Edward Fletcher, Harold Ferguson, and the flight engineer, Flight Sergeant Jenkinson.**

The following month a Blenheim crashed on the island of Rennesoy near Stavanger, after being attacked by German fighter planes. On the fortieth anniversary of the liberation of Norway on May 8th, 1945, the mayor unveiled a memorial plaque to the three crew members who were killed. Several hundred people attended the ceremony but it was so long after the event that the next of kin of the crew, Flight Sergeant P. G. Cory (pilot), Sergeant D. F. Campbell (navigator) and Sergeant F. G. Kingham (wireless operator) could not be traced.

Twenty miles north-east of Trondheim parts of a Spitfire lie at the foot of a rough stone block marking the spot where it crashed in 1942. The triangular plaque states in Norwegian that Flying Officer Frederick Ian Malcolm fell here. The plane had taken off from the Shetland Isles on a photographic reconnaissance of Trondheim and never returned. The reason for the crash remains a mystery.

Also unveiled on the fortieth anniversary of the liberation of Norway, like the one at Rennesoy, was a granite slab commemorating fourteen Allied airmen who died in February 1945. It was erected on a temporary site at Førde, the small town at the head of Staviford, north of Bergen, until its permanent place at the new airport was ready. The airmen — ten Canadians, two Australians and two from Great Britain — were part of the Dallachy Strike Wing in Scotland, flying Beaufighters as part of Coastal Command. They were attacking German shipping in the fjord. The main target was a destroyer Z-33 sheltering close under the steep side of the fjord. The Beaufighters were fired on by shore batteries, flak ships and the destroyer itself. Out of the thirty-two aircraft which set out only twenty-three returned, many badly damaged.

Part of the wreckage of yet another type of British aircraft lies in the heart of the forest near Risor in southern Norway. It was a Stirling. A memorial was erected in 1983 by former members of the Norwegian Resistance to the crew who were killed when the aircraft was shot down while dropping supplies to them.

A rare memorial to Allied airmen was built in Germany by a Hungarian refugee, Karl Frauhammer. He did it entirely as a gesture of peace. Once again this stone stands in a forest, this time at Michelbach near Heidelberg, where a Lancaster crashed. Symbols representing earth, water and the sun embellish the red sandstone memorial, as well as a piece of one of the bombs from the aircraft. A picture of the Lancaster is incorporated in the wrought iron gate with seven crosses, one for each member of the crew who died.

On the George Cross island of Malta, high above Valletta harbour, many airmen are commemorated. A marble column, rivalling the one to the Wright brothers for height, commemorates the airmen of the British Commonwealth and Empire missing from operations over southern Europe and the Mediterranean who have no known graves. A magnificent golden eagle with outspread wings surmounts the column and around the base are bronze panels bearing the names of two thousand three hundred and one airmen. The inscription on the central panel includes the following theatres of war: Malta, Gibraltar, Mediterranean, Adriatic, Tunisia, Sicily, Italy, Yugoslavia and Austria.

Even further afield in the depths of the steamy jungle of New Guinea at Evase is the Airmen's Memorial School. Air Vice-Marshal Bill Townsend of the Royal Australian Air Force was instrumental in raising the money to build the school with the help of an American pilot, Major Fred Hagesheimer, and members of the Royal Air Force Escaping

Society. It was a token of thanks to the villagers who hid them from the Japanese for four months. The first teacher was Koukika who as a boy of twelve alerted the fugitives just as the Japanese were about to enter the village. When the school opened in 1964 Major Hagesheimer and his wife went to live in the village to help with the school.

Still in the Far East but in the Philippines is a landmark which boasts the following legend:

KAMIKAZE FIRST AIRFIELD HISTORICAL MARKER

Underneath is a summary of the part played by the Japanese Air Force in World War Two reading:

THIS SPOT IS THE CENTRAL FRONTAGE OF THE VERY FIRST JAPANESE KAMIKAZE AIRFIELD OF WORLD WAR II · THE MABALACAT EAST AIRFIELD. ON 20 OCT. 1944 ADM. TAKIJIRO OHNISHI FOUNDED THE KAMIKAZE AT MABALACAT. THE FIRST TO VOLUNTEER WERE THE 24 FLIERS OF THE 201ST AIR GROUP. 1ST AIR FLEET, IMPERIAL NIPPON NAVAL AIR FORCE, UNDER CMDR. ASAICHI TAMAI, THEN STATIONED AT MABALACAT. THIS FIRST KAMIKAZE GROUP WAS CALLED THE SHIMPU SPECIAL ATTACK CORPS UNDER LT. YUKIO SEKI. THE CORPS WAS DIVIDED INTO FOUR UNITS: THE SHIKISHIMA UNIT, THE YAMATO UNIT, THE ASAHI UNIT AND THE YAMAZAKURA UNIT. AT 0725 Hrs. ON 25 OCT. 1944 THE SHIKISHIMA UNIT TOOK-OFF FROM THIS AIRFIELD LED BY LT. SEKI. HIS MEN WERE: Sgt. IWAO NAKANO, Sgt. NOBUO TANI, EM½c HAGIME NAGAMINE & EM⅔c SHIGEO OGURO. AT 1045 Hrs. ON THE SAID DATE, THE UNIT HIT ENEMY TARGETS NEAR LEYTE, LT. SEKI's PLANE HIT FIRST, BLOWING UP THE U.S. CARRIER ST. LO WHICH SANK 20 MINUTES LATER. LT. SEKI's MEN ALSO HIT AND HEAVILY DAMAGED THE U.S. CARRIERS: KALININ BAY, KITKUN BAY, SANGAMON, SANTEE, SUWANNEE & WHITE PLAINS, THIS FIRST SUCCESSFUL KAMIKAZE MISSION WAS WITNESSED, THEN REPORTED HERE BY C/wo HIROYOSHI NISHIZAWA, JAPAN's GREATEST ACE PILOT WITH 103 KILLS CONFIRMED. WAR HISTORIANS CONSIDER LT. YUKIO SEKI AS 'THE WORLD's FIRST OFFICIAL HUMAN BOMB!'

Coming forward in time, and across many miles to the Space Center at Cape Kennedy, Florida, there is plenty to see there relating to America's part in the development of aviation. But in its midst is a small circular plaque with a profile view of a man whose face is, perhaps, not very well

The signatures of Soviet cosmonauts beneath the mask of Yuri Gagarin were inscribed during a visit to the Space Center at Cape Kennedy in 1975, in connection with a joint Apollo/Soyuz test project.

known: Yuri Gagarin, the Russian cosmonaut and the first man to orbit the earth in 1961.

The most striking aviation landmark in the United States soars skywards outside the National Air and Space Museum in Washington DC. Entitled 'Ad Astra — To the stars', it immortalizes the development of aviation and space flight. It really is a magnificent structure. Made of gold coloured stainless steel, three slender fins reach a hundred feet into the sky. At the top are several steel 'starbursts' symbolising man's future goals in space.

17   INTO THE JET AGE

How flying would have developed without the Second World War is a question which can never be answered. The days of the individual designer struggling to create a complete aircraft were long gone. Technical developments meant that new models were the work of aircraft companies. During the fighting emphasis was on production but development did not stand still.

As early as 1942 a committee headed by Lord Brabazon was discussing specifications for Britain's post-war civil aircraft requirements. Six were issued, six aircraft emerged. They were the Bristol Brabazon, the Bristol Britannia, the Airspeed Ambassador, the Miles Marathon, the de Havilland Comet and the de Havilland Dove. The last one was the most successful. A two-engined feeder airliner carrying up to twelve passengers, it sold over five hundred and some are still flying.

Few aviation records were broken in the immediate post-war period, unlike the time after the First World War when aviators were ready and raring to go. However, immediately the war was over memorials associated with it began to appear and continue to do so.

The year 1958 saw the completion of St Clement Danes as the Central Church of the Royal Air Force. The beautifully proportioned church built by Sir Christopher Wren in 1682 was reduced to a shell during the London Blitz. For many years it stood derelict, a charred ruin open to the sky. When the suggestion was made that the Royal Air Force might like to restore the church for its own use the idea was greeted enthusiastically. Money poured in from all over the world. Work started in 1955 and took three years to complete.

The size of the Royal Air Force at its peak can be judged by the number of slate crests inset in the floor. Over seven hundred of them depict the badges of squadrons and units including many of those in supporting rôles such as communications and maintenance, without whom those in the front line could not operate. Around the sides are the Memorial Books containing over 125,000 names of those who have given their lives in the service of their country.

Restoration work begins on the future Central Church of the Royal Air Force in 1955.

St Clement Danes, at the end of Fleet Street by the Strand, was destroyed by fire during the major bombing raid on London on the night of May 10, 1941. Our pictures show the church burning during the raid and as it stands today.

The badges of our Commonwealth Allies encircle that of the Royal Air Force on the floor of the entrance, while in the floor of the north aisle is the insignia of the Polish Air Force. This is surrounded by sixteen of their squadron badges and again St Paul's words which are always associated with the Polish Forces: 'I have fought a good fight, I have finished my course. I have kept the faith.' The font down in the crypt was a gift from the Royal Norwegian Air Force, appropriately made of Norwegian granite.

The names of members of the Royal Flying Corps, the Royal Naval Air Service and the Royal Air Force who received the Victoria Cross are carved in the dark oak panelling near the sanctuary, a list which includes famous men such as Leonard Cheshire and Guy Gibson whose deeds are legend. Alongside them are some of the finest heroes whose names did not hit the headlines like Ian Bazalgette and Arthur Aaron, the two Pathfinders commemorated at Bexwell, Norfolk. Facing the sanctuary is a reading desk commemorating 'Sailor' Malan and other South African airmen. Adolph Malan was an Afrikaner who fought with the British, survived the war and returned to South Africa.

Behind the desk is a chair with a flying pig crest, given by the Guinea Pig Club in memory of surgeon Sir Archibald McIndoe. He performed remarkable feats of plastic surgery

These two pictures give an idea of the immense tasks that faced the restoration team when they began the restoration work in 1955 *above left*. All the bells had crashed to the ground in the fire, save one, and only the pulpit and six carved wooden cherubs were spared the conflagration. *Above right:* **The rebuilding and restoration work took three years, the final cost (in 1958 values) totalling £234,144.**

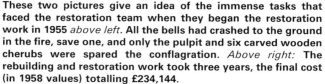

on injured servicemen who called themselves his guinea pigs and their hospital at East Grinstead was the 'sty'. Next to it, in the nave the ends of the front pews are decorated by the coats of arms of past Chiefs of the Air Staff. Their names echo pages of aviation history, most famous among them is Lord Trenchard.

The United States Air Force, always generous with their gifts, together with their families and friends gave the magnificent organ which is above the West Door. Created by Ralph Downes, it was built by Harrison and Harrison of Durham and is regarded as one of the best in London. Its black and gold decoration greatly enhances the decor of the church.

Beneath it, individual items on display mark different events, the most striking, a sword inscribed: 'The Few and to the many who helped make victory possible'. The familiar figure of Pegasus stands as a tribute to glider pilots of the war. Near it is a casket of gold, frankincense and myrrh from RAF Muharraq, Bahrain, the casket was given to St Clement Danes when the station closed in 1977.

Britain's first jet powered aircraft was commemorated in 1977. In that year, Hugh Burrows, Director of Gloster Aircraft Company from 1917 until 1966, presented a plaque commemorating the Gloster E28/39, built to take the first jet engine developed by Sir Frank Whittle. The aircraft made its first flight at RAF Cranwell, Lincolnshire, in May 1941 amid great secrecy. The two-engined Meteor, a milestone in aviation, was developed from the E28/39 and entered service with the Royal Air Force in 1944.

The memorial plaque is mounted on a pillar sited near the old runway of the Gloster Aircraft Company at Hucclecote, Gloucestershire, now part of a trading estate, and it was unveiled by Sir Arnold Hall, a close friend of Sir Frank Whittle. Among the aviation personalities at the ceremony were Battle of Britain pilot Air Vice-Marshal Denis Crowley-Milling, Group Captain Douglas Bader, Group Captain John Cunningham and Squadron Leader Neville Duke who all flew Meteors.

A second plaque exhibited in the company's reception hall has a bas-relief of the E28/39 in silver on bronze. Several workmen are shown looking on while others are lowering the engine into place with a hoist.

In the sixties and seventies aviation was enlivened by the exploits of aerobatic pilot, Neil Williams. In Strathallan Air Museum near Perth, now closed, a marble tablet, given by the French Aerobatic Society, could be seen next to a photograph of him and highlighting his career. He was born in Canada and joined the Royal Air Force in 1955, serving as

The plaque on the pillar at Hucclecote depicting the Gloster E28/39 — the first British jet aircraft — also acknowledges the contribution made by Gloster's workforce to the war effort between 1939 and 1945.

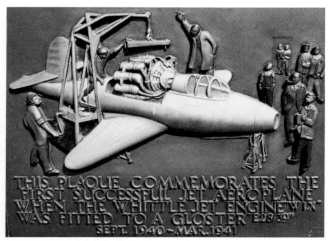

The silver and bronze plaque at Gloster's, *above*, shows the simple lines of the E28/39, designed as a flying test bed for Frank Whittle's engine.

Tribute to aerobatic pilot Neil Williams at Strathallan.

a pilot in Cyprus. Six years later he took up aerobatics in his spare time. It became an obsession. All the British aerobatic trophies went to him in 1963 and by 1965 he gained second place in the Lockheed International Competition. He left the Royal Air Force to become a test pilot at the Handley Page Company, flying in many air shows and flying the historic machines of the Shuttleworth Trust at Old Warden, Bedfordshire, where he is also commemorated. He was such a versatile pilot that he also flew sequences in films. His life was at risk many times as a test pilot and a stunt flyer. In the end, he lost it during a ferry flight bringing a vintage Heinkel bomber to Britain from Spain in bad weather.

The 'Wings for Victory' Week plaque in Harpenden Hall is placed opposite a 'Salute the Soldier' plaque, awards which were given to towns which reached a target figure during special National Savings Weeks during the war.

18   ROUND UP

Clues to aviation history turn up in the most unexpected places, even in our local public hall where an ivory coloured plaque is mounted on oak. It bears a bas-relief of St Michael, this time high above the clouds, triumphing over the devil who is represented by a serpent, and has this inscription:

WAR SAVINGS CAMPAIGN 1943 PRESENTED BY THE AIR MINISTRY IN RECOGNITION OF SUCCESSFUL ACHIEVEMENT IN WINGS FOR VICTORY WEEK.

To rise up on wings was the ambition of earlier aviators over the county of Lincolnshire. Lincoln Racecourse at West Common has a souvenir to prove that the winners of the two-thirty were not the only flyers who graced the hallowed turf. Like many racecourses, it was pressed into service during the First World War. Manufacturers needed airfields to test and adjust newly built aircraft before handing them over to the Royal Flying Corps and racecourses were ideal. Lincoln became No. 4 Aircraft Acceptance Park. Bristol F2bs, DH5s, DH6s and DH9s were a common sight racing around on the grass.

Today the racecourse is closed but the pavilion has been re-vitalised as a community centre. Nobody who enters it is left in any doubt that the Royal Flying Corps once operated there. Over the fireplace is a splendid painting of the Royal Flying Corps Wings dated 1917. 'Per Ardua — Ad Astra' is written in large gold letters underneath, the same motto adopted by the Royal Air Force.

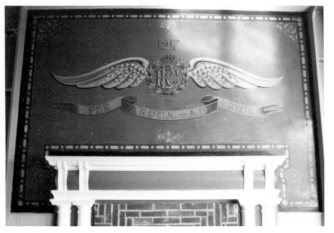

The Royal Flying Corps, whose wings span the fireplace in the old pavilion of Lincoln Racecourse at West Common, used the airfield as No. 4 Aircraft Acceptance Park. Lincoln, not now regarded as an industrial town, was a major centre of aircraft production during the First World War, turning out Sopwith Gunbuses, Handley Page 0/400s and BE2cs for delivery to West Common where they were tested and accepted by the Royal Flying Corps. After the war the airfield reverted to a racecourse which eventually closed with the buildings being put to community use.

The memorial cairn at Carn a'Choire Mhoir is close to the place where Whitley N1498 of No. 19 Operational Training Unit crashed in 1942 killing Pilot Officer J. G. Irvine, Pilot Officer J. G. Castling, Sergeant C. S. George and Sergeant C. W. Green. The memorial was dedicated on August 9th, 1984 by Squadron Leader Noel James, the station chaplain at Lossiemouth.

Twenty-five years later Wellingtons and Whitleys had replaced F2bs and DH9s as warplanes. Although Wellington crash sites are numerous, those of the Whitley seem to be most common, doubtless due to its use as a training aircraft. Sites are still being identified and marked. Over forty years passed before a cairn was erected near the summit of Carn a'Choire Mhoir south-east of Inverness where a Whitley crashed on January 6th, 1942 killing four of the crew.

On the same night another Whitley from No. 102 Squadron was lost while returning to its base at Dalton, Yorkshire, after abandoning a raid on Cherbourg due to heavy cloud. The plane caught fire. Sergeant Alexander Hollingworth, RAAF, ordered his crew to bale out. However, he and the wireless operator, Sergeant A. Buchanan, RCAF, died when the aircraft plunged into a quarry at Pogmoor, Barnsley. In January 1986 a plaque was placed in memory of the two airmen on the Royal British Legion Cottages opposite the quarry. On it a detailed picture of a Whitley is flanked by the badges of the Royal Air Forces' Association and the Royal British Legion who presented the plaque.

Young Alexander Hollingworth, great nephew of Sergeant Hollingworth after whom he was christened, at the unveiling of the commemorative plaque with his parents in 1986.

Who would have thought a crash could lead to a new airfield? Sergeant William Hodge of No. 1 Squadron based at Tangmere crashed in his Fury Fighter on Thorney Island in 1933. When the investigating team came to look at the wreckage they thought that the surrounding land was ideal for an airfield, a fact acknowledged in the last line of the inscription on a wooden plaque marking the spot: 'He died not in battle yet not in vain.'

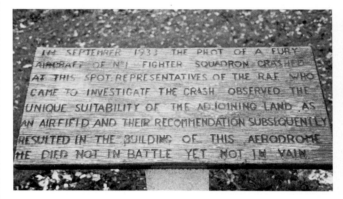

IN SEPTEMBER 1933 THE PILOT OF A FURY AIRCRAFT OF N°1 FIGHTER SQUADRON CRASHED AT THIS SPOT. REPRESENTATIVES OF THE RAF WHO CAME TO INVESTIGATE THE CRASH OBSERVED THE UNIQUE SUITABILITY OF THE ADJOINING LAND AS AN AIRFIELD AND THEIR RECOMMENDATION SUBSEQUENTLY RESULTED IN THE BUILDING OF THIS AERODROME HE DIED NOT IN BATTLE YET NOT IN VAIN

The plain wooden plaque recording the part Sergeant Hodge played at Thorney Island is now near the officers' mess of the present Army base which opened at the former airfield in 1984.

Similarly the crash of a Lancaster near Torridon, Scotland, produced major changes in the equipment and training of RAF Mountain Rescue Teams. Off course during a training exercise, the aircraft hit the side of Beinn Eighe mountain on March 14th, 1951. It took three days to locate the wreckage. The Kinloss Mountain Rescue Team was mainly National Servicemen who lacked experience and equipment. Atrocious weather conditions defeated several rescue attempts. Finally the Royal Marines reached the wreckage but were unable to begin recovering the bodies until March 30th. Service authorities were horrified at the delay, initiating immediate changes in rescue training. Teams were issued with proper equipment to enable all-weather operations.

The present Mountain Rescue Team at Kinloss tried three times to recover one of the aircraft's propellers. The hazardous position of the wreckage defeated them but in 1986 a team of RAF cadets from Cranwell aided by a helicopter from Lossiemouth succeeded in recovering one of the propellers which is now mounted on a traditional cairn.

Many landmarks are the result of joint efforts showing how a common bond of aviation enthusiasm bridges all ages. An unusual memorial at Frinton-on-Sea, in the graveyard where Church Road meets Walton Road, involved several groups as the following inscription shows:

Erected in 1978 by the Frinton and Walton branch of the RAFA to commemorate the 60th anniversary of the formation of the Royal Air Force and the 30th anniversary of the branch.

Airscrew blades were recovered in 1973 by officers and cadets of No. 308 (Colchester and Clacton) Squadron Air Training Corps from the site where a Halifax of No. 432 Squadron Royal Canadian Air Force crashed at the Naze on March 5/6th, 1945 whilst returning from an operation killing all crew. Three propeller blades from the Halifax are mounted vertically around a pillar with the Royal Air Force wings on top. It was unveiled by Colonel Bauer of the Royal Canadian Air Force in honour of the Canadian airmen.

A board at the side of the aircraft tells how both of them took part in the Falkland Islands War in 1982. They were part of the 'Black Buck' operation which was the longest bombing raid in history. The Vulcan dropped twenty-one bombs on Stanley Airport on April 30th, 1982. During the fifteen-hour, 7,860 mile return journey from Ascension Island Victor tankers provided six in-flight refuellings. The one at Waddington supplied the last one and had to provide extra fuel to avoid the Vulcan ditching in the sea four hundred miles short of Ascension. Both aircraft were in squadron service for over twenty years before being 'retired' to Waddington.

In contrast to these huge aircraft, one of the smallest memorials is at Marsworth, Buckinghamshire, on the edge of the old USAAF airfield at Cheddington. A star-shaped runway light is set into the ground in a brick alcove and dedicated to the United States Eighth Army Air Force who were stationed there for three years.

On the day I visited it, an ex-member of the US Eighth Air Force who remained nameless, arrived to see it having flown five thousand miles. He had vaguely heard about the airfield memorial and was expecting to see something more on the lines of the Statue of Liberty. For a moment he stood looking down at it, a disappointed figure in a lightweight suit, burdened with photographic equipment. Then he straightened up, smiled and drawled, 'Here we have an anti-climactic situation.'

An unusual centrepiece for a memorial to the USAAF units which served at Cheddington between 1942 and 1945 is this insignificant, yet vital, part of an airfield's furniture: a runway light. Some £10 million (probably £250 million in today's money) was spent on airfield lighting during the war, without which night operations would have been impossible.

Sometimes a memorial has a bonus for visitors. One of the best is at RAF Waddington, Lincolnshire, and well worth the short detour off the A607 to see it. At a corner of the airfield is a fine grey granite column in the style now typical of a Lincolnshire squadron memorial, this one is dedicated to No. 44 (Rhodesia) Squadron. Above the inscription is the squadron badge which appropriately has an elephant as its symbol. Rhodesia refers to the country which 'adopted' No. 44 Squadron and supported them in many ways during the war. Now it is almost overshadowed by the enormous bulk of a Vulcan and a Victor, two of the V-Bomber Force that were the mainstay of the Royal Air Force from the late fifties onwards. The delta-winged Vulcans remained in service as bombers, while the Victors were converted to tanker aircraft for refuelling others during flight.

Samuel Franklin Cody makes his first sustained fight in Britain at Swann Inn Plateau, Farnborough, on October 16th 1908.

19   THE MEN BEHIND THE MONUMENTS

The various landmarks show that controlled flight is one of the most rapid developments of all time. It progressed from short hops to space travel in less than a lifetime and there are people alive today who were born when motorised flight was still a dream.

Numerous types of aerial craft including balloons and airships are depicted on monuments. Those at Eastchurch are among the earliest showing designs which became the basis of successful machines. The various memorials and landmarks make it clear that in the early days of flying the emphasis was on records. To be first or fastest was paramount. At least three candidates claimed the first flight in Britain. Cody's memorial at Farnborough declares that his flight on October 16th, 1908 was the first sustained and powered flight in Great Britain.

Moore-Brabazon's flight at Sheppey in April 1909 was the first officially recognised flight in England by a resident Englishman and he received Aviator's Certificate No. 1 for his effort, but, after many decades, A. V. Roe was finally acknowledged to have made the first flight in Britain during a series of trials at Brooklands in 1907/8.

The period between 1903 and 1914 was an era of friendly rivalry among pioneer aviators. Distance, speed and height records were continually broken as aeroplanes developed and the pilots gained in skill. The onset of war in 1914 changed the picture from one of carefree days of flying for fun to the grim reality of air warfare.

The style of a memorial usually gives a clue to its date. Older inscriptions read 'The Great War', as there was no presentiment of what was to come. Early ones tend to have much more writing on them such as those to Charles Rolls in Monmouth and Leefe Robinson at Cuffley, and the decoration is often in classical style. Public subscription to erect them was also common, firstly because aeroplanes were a source of great wonder to many people who still thought motor cars were miracles, and later because enthusiasm generated by the national press caught the imagination of the public. Newspapers were the 'media' of the day as radio was still in its infancy and television unheard of. Aviators were the 'pop stars' of the twenties and thirties. They brought excitement into the lives of millions who battled against poverty in the years between the two world wars. Press barons offered enormous prizes for new achievements and aviators were given headline treatment in the newspapers.

After a flurry of long-distance records in the twenties and early thirties, the scene darkened over Europe. Aviation development again became dominated by military aircraft. The monoplane gained favour. Bombers became bigger and fighters faster. The expansion of the Royal Air Force is shown by the number of divisions mentioned in inscriptions. Beside Bomber, Fighter and Coastal Commands, there were less well known ones like Reserve, Training and later Ferry Command. The steady post-war contraction of the Royal Air Force has reduced this number to two home Commands, Strike and RAF Support.

New memorials are constantly appearing. Some are especially fitting like the one put up in 1987 to commemorate No. 617 Squadron at Woodhall Spa, their wartime base in Lincolnshire. Popularly known as the Dambusters, they were formed to destroy the great dams of the Ruhr and so paralyse the German armament factories. Not for them a now traditional Lincolnshire pillar. No, they have a twenty-foot-long stone dam fronted with arches nine feet high, breached by a simulated water flow of green slate emblazoned by 617's insignia — a ruptured dam — and their motto 'Apres moi le deluge'. The names of the squadron members who died in the war are engraved on six slate panels within the arches.

Almost as apt is a small reminder of the raid at the reservoir where the squadron practised. This is off the A57 road high in the Peak District's Derwent Valley. The dam with its Gothic style towers was the ideal place to practise for the raid on the Ruhr because the layout was similar. Inside the arched gateway to the dam are two memorials: one a stone tablet erected by public subscription as a tribute to the men of No. 617 Squadron and their part in the raid. Above it is a plaque commemorating the night of the raid and the 204 men of the squadron who laid down their lives during the war.

Whereas we have to rely on pictures or models to see what most early aircraft looked like, later ones have been preserved in aviation museums. In large collections such as Duxford in Cambridgeshire, it is possible to see how the shape of aircraft has gradually changed from a simple cross such as the BE2c, to those with tapered wings like a DH Dragon Rapide and through to the streamlined jets and finally Concorde.

New monuments reflect new thinking. In September 1989 a single tribute to embrace all men and women who served in British, Commonwealth and Allied Air Forces during the Second World War was unveiled on Plymouth Hoe — the impressive figure of an airman cast in bronze stands as a reminder of the vital part played by them all at a place which recalls earlier days when the freedom of the British people was threatened by the Spanish Armada.

More and more memorials are appearing in East Anglia. Outside the main gate of RAF Honington a black and gold plaque honouring the men of the 1st Strategic Air Depot USAAF was unveiled in 1987. A few miles away the market town of Thetford displays two plaques. One was placed next

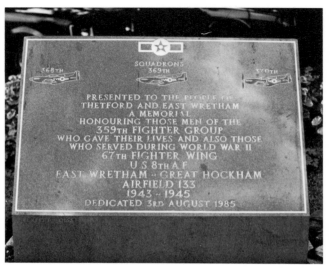

Three Mustangs depicted above the numbers 368th, 369th and 370th recall the squadrons of the 359th Fighter Group which flew Mustangs while stationed at East Wretham from 1943 to 1945. The memorial stands opposite the statue of Thomas Paine in the centre of Thetford.

The memorial at Honington records the four years when it was occupied by the men of the 1st Strategic Air Depot of the United States Army Air Force, their job being to act as quartermaster for all the airfields in their division. Honington was one of the last American airfields to be handed back to the RAF in February 1946. Now, still very much an active station, it is the home of the Tornado Weapons Conversion Unit.

to the entrance to the Arts Centre in 1980 by Czech airmen in honour of their fallen comrades. The second in polished granite commemorates the men of the 359th Fighter Group. It stands near the council offices opposite Thetford's most famous son, author Thomas Paine. Over two hundred years ago he advanced the cause of American Independence with his controversial publication *Common Sense* advocating immediate independence from Britain. He was not to know that in 1943 freedom-loving American citizens would arrive in his native Thetford to help Britain in her hour of need.

Individual airmen are not forgotten. In July 1988 the people of the town of March in Cambridgeshire honoured a brave young Australian who stayed with his doomed aircraft to prevent it from crashing on the town. Pilot Officer Jim Hocking had taken off from RAF Wratting Common, Cambridgeshire in a Stirling bomber with a full crew on a training exercise. They were all looking forward to going on leave the next day prior to a posting to an operational squadron. Suddenly one of the engines caught fire and the other three engines cut out soon afterwards. Pilot Officer

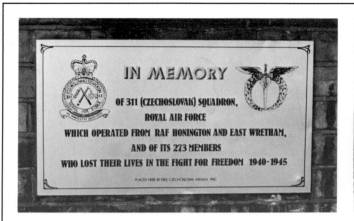

Former Czech airmen erected a plaque at the Arts Centre, Thetford, in 1980 to honour the fallen of No. 311 (Czechoslovak) Squadron, RAF. The squadron was formed in July 1940 from Czech airmen who had escaped to England, and they operated Wellingtons from RAF Honington and its satellite East Wretham. They transferred to Coastal Command and re-equipped with Liberators in 1943. At the war's end the squadron moved to Prague, some of the men remained in Czechoslovakia when the squadron was disbanded in 1946, others returned to Britain.

An atomic power station now overshadows all that remains of the wartime airfield at Bradwell Bay. A model of a Mosquito stands on its nose as a memorial to the one hundred and twenty-one Allied Airmen who died flying from the airfield, their names being engraved on plaques on either side of the aircraft.

Many memorials are cared for by the Air Training Corps. This enthusiastic band of teenagers meet to explore all aspects of aviation including its history. They are some of today's young people who are ready to answer their country's call.

Hocking ordered the crew to bale out. His last words to his Wireless Operator Stan Tebbutt were: 'Get out! I will follow when I get this thing out of here.' The plane crashed into the Royal Observer Corps post at Knight's End, away from the town, badly injuring the two men on duty. Pilot Officer Hocking's memorial, which includes the laurel wreath, which features in the Royal Observer Corps badge, is in St Wendreda's Church.

A startling reminder of the war years is at Bradwell Bay, Essex, where a model aircraft stands sentinel in honour of those who flew from RAF Bradwell Bay never to return.

The extreme youth of many pilots surprised me especially in the Services. It seems incredible that such men as First World War ace Albert Ball were so young, an indication of how many men were keen on flying from their schooldays. During the Second World War, schoolboys made excellent eyewitnesses. They were the ones who spent hours drawing aircraft, fashioning paper gliders or lying under the hedges watching the dog-fighting. They knew exactly what had come down and where.

Young men are always keen to accept a challenge. In war, their one aim is to put down the aggressor whatever the cost. Some become famous figures, others equally deserving remain unsung heroes or are commemorated in a quiet way. One such is Cyril Barton of No. 578 Squadron who earned a Victoria Cross. His courage was of the highest order. Seventy miles short of the target the control system of his Halifax was damaged and the guns put out of action. The navigator, bomb-aimer and wireless operator baled out because of a mis-interpreted signal. Pilot Officer Barton was unable to communicate with the remaining crew. He flew on and released the bombs himself. Then with the plane minus a

propeller and navigation instruments he flew back to England arriving only ninety miles north of his base at Burn in Yorkshire. He landed with only one faltering engine running and died amid the wreckage of his shattered aircraft. His name is immortalised as Barton Green, a road in his home town of New Malden, Surrey.

Sadly, airmen also die in peacetime. A plain plaque in the church at St Mawgan, Cornwall includes these words: 'Missing on a flight over the Atlantic — January 11th, 1955' and lists the names of the crews of two Shackletons of No. 42 Squadron. Both planes disappeared and they are thought to have collided. Little did they know as they took off for a routine exercise over the sea that they would never return.

The risks of flying are ever present and increasingly complex aircraft require rapid reactions. No time exists for second thoughts and inevitably losses occur. The names of today's pilots who patrol the skies for our protection are unknown. Flying is taken for granted as millions of us fly off on package holidays every year. Aerial achievements have reached a climax. Few new records are set now, but one did make the press in 1987, when two Phantom crews from No. 74 (Tiger) Squadron at RAF Wattisham, Suffolk marked the 70th birthday of the Squadron's foundation in fine style. They established a new record time for a London to Edinburgh flight, completing the three hundred and forty mile journey in twenty seven minutes and three seconds. Let their squadron mascot represent the indomitable spirit which links all flyers throughout time. Have they got a dog in a kennel, or a tame goat? No, their squadron's name is brought to life at Linton Zoo near Cambridge, where Roma, a living tiger, epitomises not only the spirit of No. 74 Squadron but of all those flyers who had the courage to take to the skies and all those who continue to do so.

Pilot Officer Cyril Barton who was awarded a posthumous Victoria Cross for his effort on March 30-31st, 1944 in continuing the flight to Nuremburg on three engines and bringing his aircraft back to Britain. He died in the crash-landing at Ryhope, County Durham, but three crew members survived.

No. 74 Squadron's mascot Roma who lives at Linton Zoo near Cambridge. She was rescued in a poor condition after another zoo closed and was due to be destroyed. Now the staff at Linton have restored her to good health but her beautiful looks belie her official rôle as the snarling tiger emblazoned on the squadron's Phantoms!

The statue of the unknown airman was unveiled on Plymouth Hoe on the fiftieth anniversary of the outbreak of the Second World War: September 3rd, 1989. The statue (dedicated to the 107,000 RAF, 84,000 USAAF and 42,200 Soviet airmen who were killed) was the brainchild of ex-Warrant Officer Jim Davis who was a rear gunner in No. 83 Squadron.

A somewhat crude but perhaps one of the most moving memorials can be seen on the summit of Great Carrs near Ambleside in the Lake District. It comprises of a wooden cross mounted atop a cairn surrounded by the massive undercarriage legs of Halifax LL505 which crashed just 20-odd feet from the summit whilst letting down through cloud, below safety height, hoping to locate its position after having become completely lost on a night navigational exercise from Topcliffe. Its trainee crew of seven from No. 1659 Heavy Conversion unit were all killed in the crash on October 22nd 1944. *TM 270009*

INDEX

Aaron VC, Flt. Sgt. Arthur 54, 127
Air Gunners' Association 51
Air Sea Rescue Service 106, 115
Air Transport Auxiliary 43
Alcock, Captain J. 8, 27, 36, 37, 38, 40, 41, 108
Alcock, Sqn. Ldr. A. 37
Aldershot 20, 67
American Cemetery Madingley 60, 100, 101
Andrew, Sgt. F. 98
Annoeullin 34
Ashton, P/O John 82
Atlantic Ferry Pilots 54
Audinghen 120

Ball VC, Cpt. Albert 33, 34, 35, 70, 111, 137
Bardney 75, 81
Barton VC, P/O Cyril 138
Bassingbourn 85, 86
Battle of Britain Memorial Flight 51, 113
Bazalgette VC, Sqn. Ldr. Ian 54, 55, 127
Ben Klibreck 96
Ben Macdui 96
Ben Mhor Assynt 94, 95
Bennett, W/Cdr. D. C. T. 54, 56, 80
Bennett, W/Cdr. J. J. 73
Bethnal Green 55, 56
Berriedale 96
Bettington, Lt. C. A. 25
Bexwell 54, 127
Biggin Hill 49, 50, 53, 104
Binbrook 78, 81, 97

Bleriot, Louis 8, 15, 16, 25, 27, 118
Bodo 122
Bomber Command 105, 111, 135
Boreham 90
Boulogne 17
Brabazon, Lord 14, 15, 19, 37, 108, 109, 126, 134
Bradwell Bay 137
Breighton 78
Bristol Aeroplane Co. 14, 20
British & Colonial Aeroplane Co. 20, 21, 23
Brompton, Caley 11
Brompton, Warneford 29, 30
Brooklands 25, 36, 65, 68, 108, 109
Brown, Lt. Arthur 101
Brown, Arthur Whitten 8, 27, 36, 37, 38, 41, 62, 108

Brown, Donald 98
Brown, Lt. Col. James Good 89
Brown, Flt. Lt. W. M. 37
Buchanan, Sgt. A. 131
Bundaberg 39, 40
Burry Port 40, 41
Bushy Park 84

Cable, S/Sgt Jay 100
Cairn Darnaw 46
Cairnsmore of Fleet 101
Calais 8, 16, 120
Caley, George 11
Camm, Sir Sydney 47, 105
Cammell, Lieut. R. A. 20
Campbell, Sgt. D. F. 123
Campbell-Black, T. 44, 45
Cannock Chase, German War Cemetery 32
Canterbury 35
Cape Kennedy 124
Cardington 38
Carn O'Choire Mhoir 131
Carsphairn 101
Castle Bromwich 66, 114, 115
Castling, P/O J. G. 131
Caudebec-en-Caux 2, 3, 4, 119, 120
Cheddington 133
Chelmsford Cathedral 90
Cheshire VC, Group Cpt. Leonard 50, 127
Cheshunt 100
Clee Hills 101
Clifden 37
Coastal Command 106, 107, 123, 135
Cocks, Charles 98
Cody, Samuel 12, 13, 14, 21, 22, 43, 47, 134
Coles, Sgt. James 123
Comet racer 9, 19, 44, 45
Coningsby 7, 51, 55, 56
Conington 88
Cory, Flt. Sgt. P. G. 123
Cox, 2nd Lt. Robert B. 100
Crackington Haven 51
Cranbrook 38
Croxton 105
Cruden Bay 26, 27, 110
Cuffley 31, 32, 134

Dale, William Philip 105
Debden 63
Dee, Sgt. T. I. 105
Demetriadi, Richard 51
Derwent Valley 135
Ditchling Beacon 51
Dolan, William 4, 88

Doran, John 98
Dormer, Sgt. John 123
Dover 8, 15, 16, 17, 28, 29, 106, 120
Dowding, Lord 4, 48, 52, 67, 68, 69, 105
Dundas, Flt. Lt. John 79
Dunning, Sq. Cdr. E. H. 43
Duxford 93, 136

Eagle Squadrons 62, 63, 84
Earhart, Amelia 40, 41, 43
Eastchurch 14, 15, 18, 19, 36, 134
East Fortune 38
East Kirkby 72, 73, 81
East Wretham 137
Ellis, 2nd Lt. John D. 100
Elmer 102, 118
Elmers End 56
Elsham Wolds 74
Elvington 77
Ely Cathedral 105

Falkson, P/O J. 122
Farnborough 13, 19, 21, 47, 134
Farringdon Road 30
Ferguson, Sgt. Harold 123
Fiske III, William Meade Lindsley 62
Fleet Air Arm 59, 60, 96, 112
Fletcher, Sgt. Edward 123
Flying Training Command 105
Flight Refuelling Ltd. 113
Førde, Norway 123
Fort de Vaux 120
Fresson, Capt. E. 43, 44, 45
Fréteval 121
Frinton-on-Sea 132

Gargarin, Yuri 124
Gale, Gen. Sir Richard 56, 57
Gander 54
Gatehouse of Fleet 96
George, Sgt. C. S. 131
Gibraltar Farm 116
Gibson VC, Guy 127
Glen Affric 101
Glenapp 106
Gordon, Louis 40
Gosport 112
Goxhill 92
Grafton Underwood 4, 7, 88, 89
Grahame-White, Claude 111
Gran, Capt. Tryggve 26, 27, 36, 110
Gravesend 50
Great Ashfield 88
Great Carrs 140

Great Dunmow 90
Great Wigborough 33
Green, Sgt. C. W. 131
Grosvenor Square 62
Guildford Cathedral 56

Hackney Marshes 109, 110
Halford, Frank 9, 44, 45
Hamel, Gustav 26
Hamilton, Capt. P. 24, 25
Harrowbeer 115, 116
Harwell 56
Hatfield 44, 45
Havilland, Geoffrey de 7, 14, 18, 19, 21, 22, 44
Hawker VC, Major L. G. 103
Hearle, Frank 18, 19
Heathrow 37, 110
Heelsum, Arnhem 122
Helvellyn 4, 39
Hemswell 83
Hendon 20, 26, 43, 47, 49, 56, 67, 70, 111
Henry, Thomas 98
Henshaw, Alex 115
Hervey. Capt. & Mrs. E. 84
Hewetson, Major A. W. 23
Hinchcliffe, Capt. W. R. 106
Hinkler, Sqn. Ldr. H. J. L. 4, 39, 40, 41, 43, 109
Hocking. P/O. J. 136, 137
Hodge, Sgt. W. 132
Holling, T/Sgt. John H. 100
Hollingworth, Sgt. A. 131
Honington 136, 137
Hornchurch 27, 32, 110
Horwich 97
Hotchkiss, 2nd Lt. E. 25
Hotton 121
Hounslow 110, 111
Hucclecote 128, 129
Hull 38, 41, 42, 43
Hull, Flt. Lt. C. B. 122
Hultengren, S/Sgt. Clare 100

Inchnadamph 95
Inverness 43, 44
Irvine P/O J. G. 131

Jackson, Leslie 46
Jankowski, T/Sgt. Stanley F. 100
Jenkinson, Flt. Sgt. 123
Johnson, Amy 41, 42, 43, 44
Jones, Capt. J. Ira 70, 71
Jones, F/O Owen 123

Kelstern 81, 83
Kent, Duke of 96
Kill Devil Hill 118
Kingham, Sgt. F. G. 123
Kings Cliffe 83, 84
Kinloss 94, 102, 132
Kinross 75
Kirkwall 43, 44
Kittyhawk 118, 119

Lane, Sgt. Ernest 82
Larkhill 20, 21, 22, 24, 25
Latham, Hubert 16, 17
Latham 47, 2, 3, 4, 119, 120
Lavenham 87
Leeds/Bradford Airport 79
Leeming, John 4
Lee-on-the-Solent 59, 60
Leuchars 75
Limburg, Belgium 82
Lincoln Cathedral 102, 105
Lincoln Racecourse 130
Lind, Bobby 98
Lippits Hill 90
Llanberis Pass 99
Loch Thom 96
Longparish 103
Loraine, Capt. 22, 25
Lorris 120
Ludford Magna 82, 97
Lunardi, Vincenzo 9, 10, 17
Luxeuil-les-Bains 120
Lydekker, Lt. A. 122

Mackay, Hon. Elsie 106
Madingley 60, 61, 101
Malan, A. G. 'Sailor' 53, 70, 71, 127
Malcolm, F/O. F. I. 123
Malmesbury Abbey 102
Malta 123
Manchester 10, 22, 36, 37, 109, 111
Mannock VC, Major E. 35, 111
March 136
Marchand, P/O Roy 50, 51
Marine Craft Section 106
Marsworth 133
Martlesham Heath 84
Maulusmillen 121
McGinley, S/Sgt William C. 100
McIndoe, Sir Archibald 127
McMullen, P/O. W. 78
McRobertson Air Race 44, 45
Mendlesham 87
Mepal 78

Merton 49, 50
Metheringham 81
Michelbach 123
Middleton St George 78
Milburn, Sgt. John 123
Military Trials 13, 20, 24, 25
Mineola 38
Minick, S. Sgt. Frank 100
Mitchell, Reginald 46, 47
Moffat 68, 69
Mollison, Capt. J. 43, 44
Monmouth 18, 134

Nantwich 101
Newark 59, 81
New Guinea 123
New Malden 138
Nicolson VC, W/Cdr. J. B. 113, 114
North Killingholme 73, 81
North Mymms 10
Northolt 59, 70
North Weald 76
Northwood 106, 107
Nottingham 33
Nuthampstead 92

Parnall, Flt/Lt Denis 51
Pathfinders 54, 55, 56, 105, 127
Pennal 97
Penmaenmawr 99
Pemberton, Harold 46
Perton 115
Philippines 124
Philpott, Archibald 46
Pilcher, Percy 11, 30
Plymouth Hoe 136, 139
Pogmoor, Barnsley 131
Polebrook 89
Polish War Memorials:
    Northolt 59
    Newark 59
    Prestwick 80
    St. Clement Danes 127
    Wigston, All Saints School 98
Porlock 100
Portal, Lord 66, 67
Postman's Park 33
Pulham 38

R33 Airship 38
R34 Airship 37, 38, 118
R38 Airship 38
R100 Airship 38
R101 Airship 38

Radlett 7
Rattlesden 91
Rawmarsh, Yorks 96
Redden, Sgt. John 82
Rennesoy 123
Rhodesian Airmen 105
Ridgewell 89
Risor 123
Robinson VC, Capt. W. Leefe 31, 32, 110, 134
Roe, Alliott Verdon 39, 108, 109, 134
Rolls, Hon. C. S. 14, 17, 18, 134
Rolls Royce 104
Romain, Pierre 17
Ropsley 105
Rosier, Pilâtre de 17
Royal Air Force Chapel, Westminster Abbey 52, 104
Royal Air Force Groups:
    No. 1 78
    No. 2 105
    No. 3 105
    No. 4 77
    No. 8 105
    No. 11 48, 49, 50, 110
    No. 18 106
    No. 38 56, 57, 113
    No. 100 105
Royal Air Force Operational Training Units:
    No. 19 94, 95, 96, 131
    No. 53 71
    No. 59 71
Royal Air Force Memorial London 4, 63, 64
Royal Air Force and
    Royal Flying Corps Squadrons:
    No. 1 29, 52, 93, 113, 132
    No. 2 28, 93
    No. 3 25, 28, 66, 93
    No. 4 28,
    No. 5 28, 67
    No. 6 103
    No. 7 93
    No. 9 75, 93, 98
    No. 10 93
    No. 12 79, 93
    No. 13 28, 110
    No. 15 93
    No. 17 93
    No. 18 93
    No. 19 93
    No. 23 93
    No. 24 103
    No. 25 93
    No. 26 93

Royal Air Force and
  Royal Flying Corps Squadrons *Continued*
No. 32 93
No. 33 74
No. 35 93
No. 39 27, 31
No. 42 138
No. 43 52, 75, 93, 113
No. 44 133
No. 54 93
No. 56 93
No. 57 72, 73, 93
No. 58 93
No. 66 50, 52
No. 71 62, 63
No. 73 50
No. 74 35, 52, 53, 70, 71, 75, 138, 139
No. 75 78
No. 77 77
No. 83 55, 56, 139
No. 85 52
No. 90 89
No. 99 93
No. 100 82
No. 101 82, 93, 97
No. 102 131
No. 103 74
No. 106 81
No. 111 75, 93, 122
No. 120 102
No. 121 63
No. 129 44
No. 132 44
No. 133 63
No. 138 116
No. 142 93
No. 153 123
No. 161 121
No. 170 83
No. 228 96
No. 234 44
No. 242 52
No. 249 52, 114
No. 263 122
No. 266 51, 83
No. 300 98
No. 302 116
No. 303 52
No. 311 137
No. 331 76
No. 332 76
No. 333 75
No. 346 77
No. 347 77

Royal Air Force and
  Royal Flying Corps Squadrons *Continued*
No. 349 83
No. 500 93
No. 501 50, 52, 93
No. 503 93
No. 504 93
No. 550 73, 121
No. 576 74
No. 578 138
No. 600 93, 111
No. 601 51, 93, 111
No. 602 93
No. 603 51, 93
No. 604 93, 111
No. 605 93, 115
No. 607 93
No. 608 93
No. 609 52, 79
No. 615 49, 50
No. 616 83
No. 617 135
No. 625 81
No. 626 79
No. 630 72, 73
Royal Australian Air Force
  No. 460 Squadron 78
Royal Canadian Air Force No. 6 Group 77
Royal Canadian Air Force Squadrons:
  No. 419 78
  No. 420 78
  No. 426 98, 99
  No. 428 78
  No. 432 132
  No. 433 73
  No. 440 96
Royal New Zealand Air Force
  No. 485 Squadron 83
Royal Observer Corps 38, 82, 137
Runnymede 58

Sadler, James 10, 11, 17
Salisbury Hall 9
Salisbury Plain 13, 20, 21,
Saffron Walden 91
St Clears 70, 71
St Clement Danes 67, 68, 126, 127, 128
St Georges Chapel, Biggin Hill 53, 104
St Kilda 94
St Mawgan 138
St Michael's Church, Coningsby 55
St Michael's Church, Highworth 30
St Paul's Cathedral 43, 62
Scallows Hall 82, 97

Scampton 73, 102, 123
Scartho 31
Schultz, Major A. 100
Scotlandwell 75
Scott, Charles 44, 45
Scott, Major G. H. 38
Scott, W. 72
Seven Barrows 7, 18, 19
Shaeffer, S/Sgt. Jack O. 100
Short Brothers 14, 15, 108
Shrewton 22
Sibsey 98
Smith, Alfred 33
Siskin, HMS 112
Somerleyton 99
Sopwith, Thomas 14, 108
Southampton 39, 40, 46, 113, 114
Spa, Belgium 121
Spaatz, Major General Carl 84
Special Operations Executive 113, 116, 120
Stalsby, F/O Samuel D. 100
Standon Green End 9, 10
Stanford Park 11
Steeple Morden 85, 86
Steyn, F/O James 94
Stonehenge 22, 23
Stultz, Wilmur 40, 41
Sudbury 87
Sultan, HMS 112
Sutton's Farm 27, 32, 110
Swingate Down 28, 29

Tangmere 50, 113, 116
Tarrant Rushton 113, 114
Tempsford 116, 117
Teynham 50
Thetford 136, 137
Thompson VC, Sgt. George 75
Thorney Island 132
Timperon, Flt. Sgt. J. B. 97
Toowoomba 54
Torridon 132
Trenchard, Lord 4, 52, 63, 65, 66, 105, 128
Trondheim 123
Tuckton 18

United States Army Air Force Groups:
  4th Fighter 63
  20th Fighter 83
  78th Fighter 93
  355th Fighter 85
  359th Fighter 136
  97th Service 83
  432nd Service 89

United States Army Air Force Corps
Continued
34th Bombardment 87
91st Bombardment 86
322nd Bombardment 91
351st Bombardment 89, 90
381st Bombardment 89
384th Bombardment 4, 88, 89
385th Bombardment 88
392nd Bombardment 91
398th Bombardment 92, 93
447th Bombardment 91
457th Bombardment 88
486th Bombardment 87
487th Bombardment 87
United States Army Air Force Squadrons:
55th 83
77th 83
79th 83
322nd 86
323rd 86
324th 86
368th 136
369th 136
370th 136
401st 86

United States Army Air Force Squadrons
Continued
508th 89
509th 89
510th 89
511th 89
532nd 89
533rd 89
534th 89
535th 89
United States Army Air Force
  65th Fighter Wing 91
Uxbridge 48, 49, 50

Valley 99, 103, 104
Vickers Company 36, 46, 108, 109

Waddington 98, 133
Waghorn, Flt/Lt H. R. D. 47
Walley, Sgt. Peter 49, 50
Wallingford 24, 98, 99
Walmer 35
Waltham 82, 121
Warneford VC, Flt. Sub-Lt. R. A. J.
  29, 30, 111
Washingborough 33

Washington 84, 124, 125
Welham Green 9, 10
Welton 102
Wendling 91
Wesley, Reginald 46
Westminster Abbey RAF Chapel 52, 104
Whitchurch 111
Whittle, Sir Frank 128, 129
Wickenby 79
Wigston, All Saints School 98
Wilding, F/O J. A. 98
Williams, Neil 128, 129
Willian 7, 24, 25
Wilson, Ian 96
Wilson, Staff Sgt. 22, 25
Wincanton 86
Windsor 26, 47
Woodhall Spa 135
Worcester Cathedral 25
Wolvercote 25
Wratting Common 4
Wright Brothers 11, 14, 118, 119, 123
Wyness Stuart, Lieut. A. 24, 25

Yeadon 79
Yelverton 115